False Christ

Will the Antichrist Claim to Be the Jewish Messiah?

By Chris White

CWM Publishing
P.O. Box 272
Ducktown TN 37326
chris@chriswhiteministries.com

False Christ: Will the Antichrist Claim to Be the Jewish Messiah? / Chris White

ISBN: 978-0-9912329-2-5

Cover image by M. S. Corley: corleyms@yahoo.com

Editing by Angie Peters, Just Words Writing & Editing Services: angiedpeters@att.net

First Edition

Further information available at the author's website: http://BibleProphecyTalk.com

Dedication

To my wife, Connie, for her steadfast love and support. To Leah Matthews and all the people who helped to shape this book by providing their thoughts and criticisms over the past few years, I couldn't have written this book without you.

Table of Contents

Preface

The purpose of this book is to reintroduce and expand upon the earliest view of the church regarding the Antichrist, a view I believe has been almost totally forgotten in recent years and one that, if true, means the deception of Satan in the end times will be far more potent that many of us have ever imagined.

My acceptance of this view didn't come lightly; in fact, you might say I came to it kicking and screaming. This is not just because I had previously been teaching another approach to the subject of the Antichrist—and many of you will understand how hard it can be to change what you have been publicly teaching—but also because I honestly didn't want the early church's beliefs to be true, for reasons I will soon discuss. However, the more I considered the idea, the more the Bible seemed to come alive. Passages that had once been obscure and difficult suddenly made perfect sense to me. Realizing I couldn't ignore this view as a possibility, I began the journey of trying to test the hypothesis.

I have written two books in preparation for this one: a verse-by-verse commentary on the book of Daniel and a commentary on Revelation 17 and 18. I initially had no plans to publish either of them as books. I had mainly wanted to study these sections of Scripture with this "new" thesis in mind to see if it could withstand the kind of scrutiny that can only come by spending a great deal of time on every single verse in question. Three years later, I am now satisfied that this view is correct. I genuinely hope this book will restart the conversation that those early church fathers began many years ago.

The interpretation of the Bible is something we should approach with godly fear and humility. Because of that, I try to err on the side of caution and avoid any type of sensational interpretations while consistently applying a "face-value" hermeneutic. That simply means that, once I've done my best to determine the meaning of a text using contextual, theological, literary, grammatical, and historical analysis, I take it at its face value. Rather than trying to argue away its meaning, I reconcile it to the rest of the Word of God and sit under its judgment.[1] If I believe that aspects of a passage are unable to be known with certainty, I will acknowledge this, and I do so quite often in this book. I hope this commitment to a sound method of interpretation will be readily apparent.

The Thesis of This Book

For the sake of clarity, I would like to begin by outlining the basic thesis of this book, so that readers can know in clear terms what I am claiming (as well as what I am not). I hope to demonstrate that the Antichrist will attempt to present himself as the Jewish Messiah and that he will try his best to appear as if he is instituting what Jewish believers know as the Messianic Age and what Christians know as the millennial reign. I hope to show in detail that his actions, according to the Bible, all seem to point to this conclusion.

Premillennial Christians and Jews have remarkably similar views as to what the world will look like during the earthly reign of the Messiah. Both Christians and Jews are awaiting the destruction of the enemies of God to occur in a great battle (Isaiah 13:6–22,

[1] http://www.solagroup.org/articles/understandingthebible/utb_0002.html

Revelation 19:11–21), to be followed by the Messianic Age, an age in which the following is expected to occur:

- The Messiah will personally rule the world with severity, “a rod of iron” (Psalm 21:8–9; Psalm 89:23; Psalm 110:5–6; Isaiah 30:14; Isaiah 60:12; Jeremiah 19:11; Daniel 2:44; Matthew 21:44; Revelation 2:26–27; Revelation 12:5).
- Jerusalem will be made the capital city of the world (Isaiah 2:1–4).
- A form of temple sacrifice will begin again (Ezekiel 43:13, 27; 45:15, 17, 20; Isaiah 56:7; 66:20–23; Jeremiah 33:18; Zechariah 14:16–21; Malachi 3:3–4).
- A worldwide pilgrimage system to Jerusalem will occur (Isaiah 60:3–22; Isaiah 18:7; Zechariah 14:16–18).

I will submit that everything we know about the Antichrist, such as his destruction of the enemies of Israel in Daniel 11:40–45, his seven-year covenant, his rebuilding of the temple and starting the daily sacrifice, his eventual stopping of the sacrifices and sitting in the temple to accept worship, his making Jerusalem the capital of the world, even his promotion by the False Prophet (who, I will argue, claims to be Elijah) points to the conclusion that his goal is to deceive the world into believing that the Messiah has come, that the Messiah is in fact God, and that He deserves the worship of the world. I will argue for this view in great detail and give special attention to objections that will inevitably come up.

I will also argue that the little-known eschatological (end-time) beliefs of the Jewish theologians, according to the Talmud and other rabbinic writings, seem to encourage Jews to accept as Messiah a man with the exact characteristics of the Antichrist. Similarly, I will argue that Islamic beliefs about the end times will cause Muslims to play a very important role in the Antichrist's rise to power.

Just to make it clear: I am not totally sure whether the Antichrist will claim to be Jesus, though I do lean toward thinking he will (see chapter 10, "Will the Antichrist Claim to be Jesus?"). As I see it, there are two possibilities regarding this issue:

1. Antichrist will claim that Jesus was not the Messiah because He didn't fulfill many of the prophecies expected of Him in the first century (such as delivering Israel from its enemies, making Jerusalem the capital city of the world, etc.).
2. Antichrist will claim to be Jesus, who has returned.

Because I'm not able to confirm my beliefs about this as conclusively as I would like, I have written this book in a way that allows for both possibilities..

Finally, one of the main criticisms I have received when talking with my peers is the accusation that this view is anti-Semitic. I take particular exception to this, because I love the Jewish people with my whole heart. I mourn when I read about the centuries of struggles and injustice that they have endured, and I rejoice when I read about their triumphs and victories. In my eight years of public ministry, I have always been an ardent defender of the Jewish cause, and some of my refutations of Jewish conspiracy theories have even been featured on Israeli national radio. I pray for and support Israel and the Jewish people, and I can assure you that anti-Semitism is as foreign to me as any other type of religious or ethnic discrimination.

The acceptance of the Antichrist as Messiah will not be limited to Jewish people by any means. In fact, Scripture tells us that this deception will affect the entire world (Revelation 13:8). It is true that the last-days events will play out in a decidedly Jewish context and many Jews will be taken in by it, but a faithful remnant of Jews and Christians will heed the warnings of Scripture and the testimony of the two witnesses and be saved. The threat of being seduced by the Antichrist is not a Jewish issue, but an issue the entire human race must face. I hope this book will help prepare all of us for it and further the cause of Jesus Christ.

> Then if anyone says to you, "Look, here is the Christ!" or "There!" do not believe it. For false christs and false prophets will rise and show great signs and wonders to deceive, if possible, even the elect. See, I have told you beforehand. (Matthew 24:23–25)

Chapter 1

The Church Fathers

The notion that the Antichrist, when he appears, would seek to convince the Jews that he is their long-awaited Messiah is unquestionably the earliest view of the church.

It should first be noted that we should never look to the church fathers alone as a way to determine the truth of Scripture. The early church fathers were fallible like all of us, and sometimes got certain points of doctrine wrong. Any doctrine must be determined solely through the study of the Scriptures. (I will spend considerable effort trying to do just that in the next chapter.)

That being said, finding agreement from the earliest writers of the Christian church can help bolster one's case and offer assurance that it isn't a new doctrine. Agreement among the church fathers can be especially noteworthy if the view was held by the majority of writers, particularly those who lived during the first few centuries after the apostles.

Of particular note among the church fathers who believed that the Antichrist would present himself as the Jewish Messiah are Irenaeus and Hippolytus. These are the two earliest church fathers to write extensively about the Antichrist. This is given extra weight when considering that both of these men can trace their teachings directly back to the apostle John through Polycarp, who was a disciple of John, who, in turn, discipled Irenaeus, who taught Hippolytus.

Some of the other church fathers I would include here are Tertullian, John Chrysostom, Cyril of Jerusalem, John Damascene, Rufinus of Aquileia, Sulpicius Severus, Victorinus of Pettau, and Methodius of Olympus. I suspect there would be many more names to add to this list if we knew what more of them thought about the Antichrist. But, unfortunately, very few church fathers wrote extensively about their views on this point.

I will start with a few quotes from the writings of Hippolytus, not simply because he was one of the first to mention the Antichrist in his writings, but also because he wrote more about eschatology than any of the others:

> Christ arose from among the Hebrews, and he [the Antichrist] will spring from among the Jews.[2]
>
> For in every respect that deceiver seeks to make himself appear like the Son of God.... The Saviour was circumcised, and he [the Antichrist] in like manner will appear in circumcision [He will be Jewish].[3]
>
> But seeing now that we must make proof of what is alleged at greater length, we shall not shrink from the task. For it is certain that he is destined to spring from the tribe of Dan.[4]

---

[2] Pseudo-Hippolytus of Rome (1886). *A Discourse by the Most Blessed Hippolytus, Bishop and Martyr, on the End of the World, and on Antichrist, and on the Second Coming of Our Lord Jesus Christ*, S. D. F. Salmond, trans. In A. Roberts, J. Donaldson & A. C. Coxe (eds.), *The Ante-Nicene Fathers,* Volume V: *Fathers of the Third Century: Hippolytus, Cyprian, Novatian,* Appendix (A. Roberts, J. Donaldson & A. C. Coxe, eds.) (247). Buffalo, NY: Christian Literature Company.

[3] Ibid.

[4] Pseudo-Hippolytus of Rome, 246.

Hippolytus states not just that the Antichrist will "spring from among the Jews," but also that he believed Antichrist would specifically come from the tribe of Dan. Although Hippolytus may have had "pet theories" about the Antichrist—like this theory that he will be from the tribe of Dan, which may or may not be accurate—he did *not* base his belief about the Jewishness of the Antichrist on his "pet theories." Instead, he used them only to support and bolster the case of his main thesis, which he and other church fathers derived from more common places like Daniel 11, John 5:43, 2 Thessalonians 2, and others.

Hippolytus is not the only church father who directly stated that he believed the Antichrist would be ethnically Jewish. There are a number of others:

> Antichrist will be possessed by Satan and be the illegitimate son of a Jewish woman.—John Chrysostom

> Even the Antichrist will enter Jerusalem, where he will enthrone himself in the temple as a god (even though he will be an ordinary man of the tribe of Dan to which Judas Iscariot also belonged).—Methodius of Olympus

The following quotes also demonstrate the prevalent view of the church fathers that the Antichrist will seek to convince the Jews that he is their Messiah:

> The Jews accordingly did not receive the Lord Jesus Christ who was the Son of God and God, but receive the impostor who calls himself God. For that he will assume the name of God, the angel teaches Daniel, saying these words, Neither shall he regard the God of his fathers.

> Who opposeth and exalteth himself above all that is called God or that is worshipped, so that he sitteth in the temple

of God, shewing himself that he is God; in the temple of God he said; not our temple, but the old Jewish temple. For he will come not to us but to the Jews: not for Christ or the things of Christ: wherefore he is called Antichrist.

But in a peculiar and special sense he who comes at the consummation of the age is called Antichrist…he will come to refute the impious Jews. For the Lord said to them: I am come in My Father's name and ye receive Me not: if another shall come in his own name him ye will receive.—John Damascene

The Lord also spoke as follows to those who did not believe in Him: "I have come in my Father's name, and ye have not received Me: when another shall come in his own name, him ye will receive," calling Antichrist "the other," because he is alienated from the Lord. This is also the unjust judge, whom the Lord mentioned as one "who feared not God, neither regarded man," to whom the widow fled in her forgetfulness of God,—that is, the earthly Jerusalem,—to be avenged of her adversary. Which also he shall do in the time of his kingdom: he shall remove his kingdom into that [city], and shall sit in the temple of God, leading astray those who worship him, as if he were Christ.—Irenaeus of Lyons

Antichrist, the son of perdition will be born in Corozain, will be brought up in Bethsaida and shall begin to reign in Capharnaum, according to what Our Lord Jesus said in the Gospel: "Woe to thee Corozain…woe to thee Bethsaida…and thou Capharnaum that art exalted up to heaven, thou shalt be thrust down to hell." (Luke, 10:13) Antichrist shall work a thousand prodigies on earth. He will make the blind see, the deaf hear, the lame walk, the

> dead rise, so that even the Elect, if possible, shall be deceived by his magical arts. Puffed up with pride, Antichrist shall enter in triumph the city of Jerusalem and will sit on a throne in the Temple to be adored as if he were the Son of God. His heart being intoxicated with arrogance, he will forget his being a mere man, and the son of a woman of the tribe of Dan.—Zenobius of Florence

It should be mentioned that there was a minority view among the church fathers that the Antichrist would be Nero, the Roman Emperor, who by that time had already been killed. But those who believed he would be the Antichrist argued that he would rise from the dead at some point. Interestingly, even those church fathers who believed the resurrected Nero would be the Antichrist also believed he would still have to convince the Jews that he was their Messiah.

The relatively few men who argued this point came up with imaginative ideas of how this scenario could come about. What I would like to draw your attention to is the fact that they went to the trouble to argue such an improbable scenario about how Nero could convince Jews that he was the Messiah, and how that shows they took for granted that the Antichrist had to be a Messiah to the Jews:

> Now that one of the heads was, as it were, slain to death, and that the stroke of his death was directed, he speaks of Nero. For it is plain that when the cavalry sent by the senate was pursuing him, he himself cut his throat. Him therefore, when raised up, God will send as a worthy king, but worthy in such a way as the Jews merited. And since he is to have another name, He shall also appoint another name, that so the Jews may receive him as if he were the Christ. Says Daniel: "He shall not know the lust of women,

> although before he was most impure, and he shall know no God of his fathers: for he will not be able to seduce the people of the circumcision, unless he is a judge of the law." Finally, also, he will recall the saints, not to the worship of idols, but to undertake circumcision, and, if he is able, to seduce any; for he shall so conduct himself as to be called Christ by them.—Victorinus of Pettau

To restate the importance of this point: The fact that these church fathers who argued that Nero would be the Antichrist felt compelled to concoct a scenario in which a resurrected Nero takes on a Jewish name and becomes a "judge of the law" shows how entrenched or non-negotiable the idea that the Antichrist must at least claim to be Jewish was in the early church. There is no other reason to argue for such an unlikely series of events.

Other early church fathers like Tertullian and Lactantius[5] believed that the Antichrist would be Jewish, yet still wanted to incorporate the view that Nero would play a role in some way. Tertullian envisioned the scenario this way:

> The Goths will conquer Rome and redeem the Christians; but then Nero will appear as the heathen Antichrist, reconquer Rome, and rage against the Christians three years and a half. He will be conquered in turn by the Jewish and real Antichrist from the East, who, after the defeat of Nero and the burning of Rome, will return to Judea, perform false miracles, and be worshipped by the Jews.

---

[5] Christian Classics Ethereal Library. "ANF04. Fathers of the Third Century: Tertullian, Part Fourth; Minucius Felix; Commodian; Origen, Parts First and Second," June 1, 2005. Http://www.ccel.org/ccel/schaff/anf04.v.ii.lxxxi.html.

I suggest that of the relatively few church fathers who wanted to expand on what I might call the "pop" view of the day—that Nero would be involved in the last days—many still did not let that take away from their opinion that the Antichrist would be a false Jewish messiah. Instead, they came up with various ways to make both lines of thinking work together.

I think it can safely be said that the early church believed the Antichrist would be Jewish, or at least that he would need to pretend to be Jewish in order to convince the Jews that he was their Messiah.

Why Did They Believe This?

Why did the early church fathers believe so strongly that the Antichrist would be a false messiah to the Jews? We will now look at the Scriptures they quoted in support of their beliefs about this. Since I will spend a lot of time in later chapters discussing these verses (and a number of others), I will refrain from commenting on them here, and I will simply list some of the passages the early church fathers have cited as support for their belief. To restate my goal, please note that some of these passages make a stronger case than others. Also, the church fathers have left out other verses that I think apply. I am simply constructing a list of the verses the church fathers used, and at this point, I am doing so without judgment as to their validity:

> I have come in My Father's name, and you do not receive Me; if another comes in his own name, him you will receive. (John 5:43)
>
> Neither shall he regard the God of his fathers. (Daniel 11:37)

Wilt thou yet say before him that slayeth thee, I am God? but thou shalt be a man, and no God, in the hand of him that slayeth thee. Thou shalt die the deaths of the uncircumcised by the hand of strangers: for I have spoken it, saith the Lord GOD. (Ezekiel 28:9–10)

And he shall plant the tabernacles of his palace between the seas in the glorious holy mountain; yet he shall come to his end, and none shall help him. (Daniel 11:45)

Thou shalt not be joined with them in burial, because thou hast destroyed thy land, and slain thy people: the seed of evildoers shall never be renowned. Prepare slaughter for his children for the iniquity of their fathers; that they do not rise, nor possess the land, nor fill the face of the world with cities. (Isaiah 14:20–21)

…Who opposes and exalts himself above all that is called God or that is worshiped, so that he sits as God in the temple of God, showing himself that he is God. (2 Thessalonians 2:4)

Therefore when you see the "ABOMINATION OF DESOLATION," spoken of by Daniel the prophet, standing in the holy place (whoever reads, let him understand), then let those who are in Judea flee to the mountains. (Matthew 24:15–16)

Then he shall confirm a covenant with many for one week. (Daniel 9:27a)

Woe to you, Chorazin! Woe to you, Bethsaida! For if the mighty works which were done in you had been done in Tyre and Sidon, they would have repented long ago, sitting in sackcloth and ashes. But it will be more tolerable for

> Tyre and Sidon at the judgment than for you. And you, Capernaum, who are exalted to heaven, will be brought down to Hades. (Luke 10:13–15)

> Dan shall be a serpent by the way, A viper by the path, That bites the horse's heels So that its rider shall fall backward. (Genesis 49:17; see also Jeremiah 8:16)

In the next chapter, I will add quite a few more verses to this list and begin to lay out the case that at least some argue strongly that the Antichrist will present himself as the Jewish Messiah..

Chapter 2

Biblical Support

There are certain verses the church fathers used to demonstrate their belief that the Antichrist would claim to be the Jewish Messiah that I believe are valid, and there are others that I think are inconclusive, and probably shouldn't be considered proof texts for the argument. I will begin with a number of passages that make a good case that the Antichrist will present himself as the Jewish Messiah, and I will conclude this chapter by discussing some of the verses that I don't think are being used responsibly to bolster the case.

Daniel 11:37

> He shall regard neither the God of his fathers nor the desire of women, nor regard any god; for he shall exalt himself above them all. (Daniel 11:37)

This verse is an important piece of the puzzle, because it is one of the few that argues not just that the Antichrist will be accepted as the Jewish Messiah, but that he really will be Jewish and not simply a pretender. This verse is interpreted in different ways, depending on a person's preconceived notions about the ethnicity of the Antichrist. If one has a view other than the Jewish Antichrist view, the phrase, "God of his fathers," must be interpreted to refer to "gods," plural—i.e., pagan deities as opposed to "God," singular—i.e., Yahweh. Even certain Bible translations have the *g* in "god" as lowercase, and feature an *s* at the end (making the word "gods" and not "God") to make it seem as if Yahweh is not in view here. I have heard commentators say things like: "In the Hebrew, 'elohim' is plural in this case," but such statements are either ignorant of Hebrew grammar or dishonest.

Take Arnold Fruchtenbaum's statement on this verse, for example: "Any student of Hebrew would see from the original Hebrew text that the correct translation should be 'the gods of his fathers' and not the 'God of his fathers.'"[6]

This is simply not true.

Dr. Michael Heiser is more than "any student" of Hebrew, having a PhD in Hebrew Bible and Semitic languages. He points out the fallacy of Fruchtenbaum's statement by saying flatly that "elohim can be either singular or plural depending on context."[7]

Heiser goes on to give examples of how to determine whether "elohim" is singular or plural. He says the word "elohim" or "god" in Hebrew is a lot like the word "sheep" or "deer" in English; it can be singular or plural, depending on the situation. For example, in the sentence, "The sheep <u>are</u> lost," we know that the usage of "sheep" is plural. However, in the sentence, "The sheep <u>is</u> lost," we know that "sheep" indicates the singular.

The same is true with "elohim" in Hebrew; that is, we cannot determine whether it is supposed to be plural or singular without looking at the context.

---

[6] Arnold G. Fruchtenbaum. In *The Nationality of the Anti-Christ,* 17–18, n.d.
[7] Dr. Michael Heiser. *Some Notes on the Word "Elohim,"* n.d. http://www.sitchiniswrong.com/dc101elohim.pdf.

Dr. J. Paul Tanner, also a Hebrew expert, agrees with Heiser and adds another point in favor of this being a reference to Yahweh in his class notes on Daniel 11: "The Hebrew term Elohim can be translated as 'God' or 'gods.' While either translation is grammatically correct, we should observe that the expression 'the God of his fathers' is a commonly used phrase in the OT to refer to Israel's covenant God, Yahweh, who had long associated Himself by covenant with the 'fathers' of the nation."

Tanner goes on to reference a number of instances when the Hebrew phrase, "God of his fathers," refers to Yahweh: Genesis 31:29, 46:1, 3; Exodus 3:16; 2 Kings 21:22; 1 Chronicles 28:9; Jeremiah 19:4; and Daniel 2:23.

There are more verses than these, too, including: "Now when he was in affliction, he implored the LORD his God, and humbled himself greatly before **the God of his fathers"** (2 Chronicles 33:12, emphasis added).

Think of how damaging that point is to Fruchtenbaum's argument. He says that "any student" of Hebrew would know that "elohim" is plural in Daniel 11:37, yet in other instances in Scripture, the same phrase is translated as singular, where it is quite clear that Yawheh, not pagan gods, is in view, while, conversely, the Hebrew phrase is *never* used to refer to pagan gods!

Joel Richardson, author of *The Mideast Beast* and a proponent of the Islamic Antichrist theory, somewhat ironically agrees with the idea that this phrase is speaking about Yahweh and not pagan gods, though he is trying to make the case that the Antichrist will be a Muslim. He asserts that when Scripture says "he" will not regard the "God of his fathers," it is a reference to how an Islamic person's lineage ultimately would go back to Abraham through Ishmael.

This, too, would have problems, because, like Fruchtenbaum's view, it is unprecedented. There is no indication of any usage of the phrase "God of his fathers" in the Bible to refer to anyone except Jews.

The "fathers" are a very distinct group of people when used in this context. Often, they are even named as Abraham, Isaac, and Jacob. The very idea that multiple "fathers"—plural, not singular—are in view in this phrase is an argument against this idea because, in Richardson's view, there is only one father who could be said to be part of Ishmael's lineage, and that is Abraham. So, the phrase "God of his Fathers" could not be theologically accurate.

Abraham's son Isaac is how the patriarchal covenant line progresses—not thorough Ishmael. It is highly doubtful, then, that Scripture would use the phrase "God of His fathers" to refer to someone outside the covenant line of Abraham, Isaac, and Jacob.

John 5:43

Another common verse used by the church fathers to suggest that the Antichrist would be received by the Jews as their Messiah—which I agree with—is found in John 5:43: "I have come in My Father's name, and you do not receive Me; if another comes in his own name, him you will receive" (John 5:43).

In John 5, when Jesus is speaking to the Jewish leadership about their rejection of Him, He makes several claims about His role during the end times. He says that He will raise the dead in the last days, and that He is the one who will ultimately judge everyone in that day. If John 5:43 is a reference to the Antichrist, then it means that the Jewish leadership, who rejected Jesus, will accept the Antichrist. If that is true, then this would argue strongly that the

Antichrist must at least claim to be Jewish in order to be accepted as the Jewish Messiah.

I will suggest several reasons Jesus means the Antichrist here and not some other Messianic pretender when He says "another." For one thing, the "receiving" spoken of here is clearly being compared to the type of reception that Jesus wanted from the Jewish leadership for Himself. The word for "receive" in the Greek here is *lambanō,* which is often used in the following context: "But as many as received [lambanō] Him, to them He gave the right to become children of God, to those who believe in His name" (John 1:12).

Another reason the Antichrist is probably in view in John 5:43 is that it seems unlikely Jesus would point to one specific person as being the one they would receive instead of Him—unless it was the Antichrist.

We know that there is no record of a false messiah who was received by the leaders of the Jews or by any other Jews of this exact time period, though there were false messiahs who would turn up in the coming centuries. In my opinion, however, none of these messianic claimants were significant enough or widely accepted enough to warrant a singling-out of one over another by Jesus. It would seem that the "one they would receive" is not only exceptional in some way, but the phrase suggests the sense of the "one" being the last one they would receive *because of the way that this was spoken.* The fact that Jesus was concerned that the people of Israel would receive a false messiah in the last days is clearly seen in Matthew 24: 5 and 24.

The view that the Antichrist is in view in John 5:43 is accepted by many conservative scholars, including one who even adds the name "one who comes in his own name" to the list of the names of the Antichrist.[8]

"One who comes in his own name" is an appropriate name for the Antichrist that has a lot of supplemental scriptural support. The idea of coming in his own name could be a reference to the Antichrist being said to exalt himself above the name of God (2 Thessalonians 2:4; Daniel 11:36). This is in direct contrast to the attitude of Jesus, who came in the "name of the Father," and it is almost certainly the reason Jesus words this phrase the way He does in John 5:43—that is, to indicate to the Jewish leadership and to us that the Antichrist is in view.

This verse does not explicitly show that the Antichrist will be ethnically or religiously Jewish, but it does say that the Jews will "receive" the Antichrist. One could argue that, of all the Messianic prophecies the Jews might be able overlook, they would never accept a Messiah who was not Jewish or who did not at least claim to be.

The Seven-Year Covenant

> Then he shall confirm a covenant with many for one week; But in the middle of the week He shall bring an end to sacrifice and offering. (Daniel 9:27a)

Here in the last verse of Daniel chapter 9, we have a reference to the Antichrist making some kind of covenant with many people. This verse gives weight to the thesis that the Antichrist will claim to be the Jewish Messiah. Even until very recently, I've assumed

[8] In John's gospel, he is probably referred to as "the one coming in his own name." *Grace Journal*, vol. 4 (Winona, Indiana: Grace Seminary, 1963)(2) (26).

that this verse was referring to a "seven-year peace agreement." It has become so common for people to refer to this verse as a peace treaty of some sort that I confess I sort of took it for granted.

However, there is no reason to think this covenant is speaking of a peace treaty. In all the Bible versions I have available to me though Bible software and the Internet (a considerable number), the word "peace" is not mentioned or even implied. In addition, I suggest that whatever this covenant is that the Antichrist makes must be a covenant that was already in place, based on the underlying Hebrew text.

I believe this verse is referring to the Antichrist trying to fulfill the modern Jewish expectations of a "new covenant" that the Messiah will make in the last days. This concept is detailed in many places in the Old Testament, but a notable one is in Jeremiah 31:31, which states: "Behold, the days are coming, says the LORD, when I will make a new covenant with the house of Israel and with the house of Judah."

Both Christians and Jews believe this verse is messianic, but their two views of this "new covenant" are vastly different. The Jews believe this means that when the Messiah comes, He will reconfirm the covenant they already had; that is, the Messiah will make it possible for them to once again abide by the laws given by Moses, especially regarding the daily sacrifices in the temple. The Jewish view of the phrase "new covenant" is no more than a renewed national commitment to abide by God's laws.

Uri Yosef, PhD, a Jewish scholar concludes his paper called "Will the Real New Covenant Please Stand Up?" this way: "It is evident that Jeremiah's use of the term ריתִבְּ חֲדָ הָשׁ , a new covenant, does not involve the replacement of the (eternal) Torah by the New

Testament. Rather, it signals a renewal of the original Sinai Covenant."[9]

JewsForJudaism.org states: "Jeremiah's 'new covenant' is not a replacement of the existing covenant, but merely a figure of speech expressing the reinvigoration and revitalization of the existing covenant."[10]

Keep in mind that Uri Yosef and the writers of the article in JewsForJudaism.org, like many Jewish people, would agree that this renewing of the Mosaic covenant will happen when the Messiah comes. They believe that one of the ways He will do this—probably the most important way—is by reestablishing the sacrificial system.

Interestingly, this is exactly what Daniel 9:27 states with the words "he shall 'confirm a covenant'" (New King James Version, NKJV). This phrase, "confirm a covenant," is very interesting, and the Hebrew words are apparently difficult to translate into English. Note a sample of how differently it is translated in popular versions of the English Bible:

> **NET Bible (NET):** "He will confirm a covenant."
> **English Standard Version (ESV):** "And he shall make a strong covenant."
> **King James Bible (KJV):** "And he shall confirm the covenant."

---

[9] Uri Yosef, PhD. Jeremiah 31:30–36[31-37]1 Will the Real "New Covenant" Please Stand Up! 2001–2011 for the Messiah Truth Project.

[10] Gerald Segal. "Is Jeremiah's 'New Covenant' (Jeremiah 31:31–34) a Prophecy Fulfilled by the New Testament?", n.d., http://jewsforjudaism.org/knowledge/articles/jeremiah/is-jeremiahs-qnew-covenantq-jeremiah-3131-34-a-prophecy-fulfilled-by-the-new-testament/.

Young's Literal Translation (YLT): "And he hath strengthened a covenant."

Notice that it isn't just the words, but their core meaning, that vary. In the NET translation, "he" is confirming an *already existing* covenant; in the ESV, "he" makes a *new* strong covenant; in the KJV, "he" confirms *the* covenant, suggesting it is the Mosaic covenant; and in the YLT, "he" is strengthening an *already-existing covenant*. Of the nineteen versions of the Bible I checked, eleven have the Antichrist confirming or strengthening an already-existing covenant as opposed to making a new covenant altogether.

The obvious question is: Which one is right? I will add a discussion about the details of this linguistic problem in the footnotes,[11] but I believe the original Hebrew expresses a confirming or strengthening of an already-existing covenant. The idea of the covenant being strengthened comes from the fact that the Hebrew word sometimes translated "confirm" carries the meaning of making something strong. I would even suggest that this covenant was meant to be understood as *the* covenant, i.e., the Mosaic covenant. Some translations, like the KJV, even render the word "a" as "the," which suggests a reference to a particular, preexisting covenant. Contextually, that must be the Mosaic covenant.

There seems to be confirmation that we're on the right track with this idea, because the second part of Daniel 9:27 says, "But in the middle of the week He shall bring an end to sacrifice and

---

[11] And he shall confirm the covenant—literally, "he shall make strong"—והגביר vehîgebîyr. The idea is that of giving strength, or stability; of making firm and sure.—*Barnes Notes on the Bible* (Daniel 9:27). (See also the following footnote.)

offering," as if to suggest that it is obvious that the covenant being strengthened began by starting the daily sacrifices. This verse is contrasting these two ideas; it's like the verse is saying: "he confirms the covenant [which started the daily sacrifices], but then [three and a half years later] he stops the sacrifices." The words presuppose that the reader understands the covenant began with the daily sacrifices restarting.

If this is speaking of the Antichrist trying to fulfill the Jewish expectations of Jeremiah 31's "New Covenant," then the singling out of the daily sacrifice here and in other places where this event is mentioned is pretty interesting, because, to put it simply, without the daily sacrifice it is very difficult, if not impossible, to truly keep the Mosaic covenant. It is the first and most important of all sacrifices to the Jews, it made daily atonement for their collective sin, and it's believed that this sacrifice must start again for God's blessing to rest in its fullness on the Jewish people. In the Jewish mind, the reinstatement of the daily sacrifices is tangible proof that the Messiah has come and Jeremiah 31:31 has come true.

If this scenario is true, the idea that the Antichrist will announce a seven-year covenant, as opposed to announcing an eternal covenant, is absurd. He would not say, "Hey, everyone, I'm the Messiah, and now you have a new covenant, but it's really not eternal; it's only going to last seven years." Here again, I think we are victims of modern Bible prophecy teaching. Scripture never says that he will say that he is setting up a seven-year covenant; it only says that the covenant will last seven years. In fact, according to a lengthy study on grammar by the *Pulpit Commentary,* linked in the footnotes, the underlying Hebrew suggests this, too. That study concludes by translating that part of the verse this way: "The covenant shall prevail for many during one week."[12]

So, it seems clear that the seven-year time frame will not be announced to the people who are agreeing to it. The Antichrist will in all probability say that this will be an eternal covenant. The mentioning of the seven years is therefore just God telling us how long this false covenant will really last. Note also that Scripture says it will continue to last the entire seven years. It won't go away at the midpoint. Only the daily sacrifices will be taken away, a point we will discuss at length later in the section on the "Abomination of Desolation."

I believe the covenant the Antichrist makes is an argument in favor of the case that he will claim to be the Jewish Messiah. The Jews are wholeheartedly expecting the Messiah to do the exact thing Daniel 9:27 is saying the Antichrist will do—that is, confirm a covenant and start the daily sacrifices. We can be sure that whoever does this will be looked at as the Messiah by the Jews as well as by many Christians, who may see this as the beginning of the millennial reign of Christ.

---

[12] The clause, "the covenant shall be strong (δυναστεύσει) upon many," is a doublet of the clause, "when he shall confirm the covenant to many weeks." The clause, "and after seven and seventy times and sixty-two years," is a doublet of the beginning of the twenty-sixth verse; "Till the end of the war, and the desolation shall be taken away," is an alternative version of the last clause of the twenty-sixth verse. When those extraneous elements are got rid of, we have left a rendering of the twenty-seventh verse, which may afford us light as to the text. "The covenant shall be strong upon many" is a possible rendering of the Hebrew (see Psalm 12:5).—*Pulpit Commentary* (Daniel 9:27).

The False Prophet

Not too many places in Scripture discuss this person who will come to be known as the False Prophet, but the information we do have about him strongly supports the idea that the Antichrist will claim to be the Jewish Messiah.

I am convinced that the False Prophet will claim to be Elijah the prophet.

Most of us know that the prophet Elijah, who was carried up to heaven in a whirlwind, was prophesied to come back to prepare the way for the Messiah.

> "Behold, I will send you Elijah the prophet before the coming of the great and dreadful day of the LORD. (Malachi 4:5)
>
> The voice of one crying in the wilderness: "Prepare the way of the LORD; Make straight in the desert a highway for our God." (Isaiah 40:3)

The idea of Elijah coming back is so important in Jewish religious culture, it is hard to imagine that any Messiah figure could be considered by the Jews unless he had a sidekick who claimed to be Elijah.

We could spend quite some time talking about Jewish traditions regarding Elijah—things like setting out a chair for him during circumcision ceremonies or putting out a cup for him at the Passover meal. Even the Havdalah, a hymn that concludes every Sabbath, makes reference to Elijah's return: "Elijah the Prophet,

Elijah the Tishbite, let him come quickly, in our day with the Messiah, the son of David."[13]

We are given strong evidence that the False Prophet will claim to be Elijah because the only prophetic "sign" he is specifically mentioned to do is call down fire from heaven (Revelation 13:13).

This apparent miracle is crucially important. To anyone else in the world, calling down fire from heaven would be a neat trick but nothing more. But to a Jew, a prophet calling down fire from heaven is almost the same as declaring himself to be Elijah, the only prophet to perform such an interesting action, which he did three times. Combine this with the fervent Jewish expectation of Elijah's return, and it's easy to see that by this one act, the False Prophet is setting himself up as Elijah. Once the False Prophet has convinced the people that he is Elijah, he will be expected to point to the true Messiah. These miracles appear, then, to be a means by which to fulfill his primary duty of promoting the Antichrist (Revelation 13:12).

It is interesting that, around the same time in Jerusalem, the two witnesses, one of whom may very well be the real Elijah, will be able to stop the rain (Revelation 11:5). Stopping the rain is another major miracle Elijah performed. If one of these witnesses is Elijah, I wish I could say that he will be getting more attention than the fake one (the False Prophet). But, based on the joyful reaction of the people of Jerusalem when the two witnesses are killed, it seems that it is not to be. The people in Jerusalem celebrate and give gifts to one another when the two witnesses are killed (see Revelation 11:10).

---

[13] Joesph Telushkin. *Jewish Literacy*. (New York: William Morrow, 2001).

It may seem that the two witnesses have the False Prophet out-"Elijahed," because they throw fire around and stop the rain as Elijah did, whereas the false Elijah is only calling down fire from heaven. However, there are some interesting reasons to believe that the False Prophet will do one of the other major miracles of Elijah—probably the most impressive of all: seem to raise someone, namely, the Antichrist, from the dead. I will explain this in detail later in the chapter about "Jewish Eschatology" (see chapter 5), but if the False Prophet does raise the dead, call down fire from heaven, and point to the Messiah, then it will be a very strong deception indeed for any Jew waiting for Elijah.

So, the acts of the False Prophet seem to be his attempt to pass himself off as the long-awaited, returning Elijah. Since we know the False Prophet uses his powers for the sole purpose of directing people to the Antichrist, it seems obvious that he is therefore going to claim that the Antichrist is the Messiah.

I will discuss the False Prophet in more detail in chapter 6, "Islamic Eschatology," as well as in the appendix.

Daniel 11:45

> And he shall plant the tents of his palace between the seas and the glorious holy mountain. (Daniel 11:45, NKJV).

This verse comes at a very interesting time in the book of Daniel—right after the Antichrist has defeated most of the enemies of Israel, like Egypt and an Arab coalition. (We will talk more about this in chapter 3, "The Wars of the Antichrist.") The verse also comes right before the abomination of desolation and the beginning of the persecution that follows it (Daniel 12:1). So the Antichrist setting up his palace tents here occurs right around the midpoint of the seventieth week of Daniel.

This verse, like the others we've been looking at, helps bolster the case that the Antichrist will seek to present himself as the Jewish Messiah. One of the reasons is because of the placement of his headquarters, which I believe this verse is saying will be in Jerusalem, right in front of the rebuilt temple.

The version I quoted above is from the NKJV, the one I am primarily using for this book. But if we were to only look at the NKJV translation of this verse, it would be easy to miss the location of the Antichrist's headquarters, because it gives the impression that he sets up his palace tents between the Mediterranean Sea and the glorious holy mountain (speaking of Mt. Zion in Jerusalem). This would lead us to believe that the site is at some location between Jerusalem and the Mediterranean Sea. However, the NKJV has a very different translation of this verse than the original KJV, and it is one of the few occasions when I feel the NKJV, though trying to improve upon the KJV, includes a big mistake. I submit that the translators probably included this error more because of their personal beliefs rather than because of the underlying Hebrew meaning.

This is how the original KJV renders this verse: "And he shall plant the tabernacles of his palace between the seas **in** the glorious holy mountain" (emphasis added).

This translation offers a totally different placement for the Antichrist's palace tents: "between the seas in the glorious holy mountain." This translation is agreed upon by a number of very good modern translations, like the NET Bible and the International Standard Version (ISV), as well.

The phrase "between the seas" is a reference to the Mediterranean Sea and the Dead Sea—a point that is also footnoted in the NET

Bible. If you look at a map of Israel, you will find that Jerusalem is located in between the Dead Sea and the Mediterranean Sea.

The KJV says the palace tents will be “in” the holy mountain, whereas others translate this word as “facing” the holy mountain (ISV) or as being “toward” the holy mountain (NET). Either way, the intent seems to be that the palace tents are very close to the Temple Mount.

Below are a few translations of this verse; note that if the first part of the verse (about the palace tents being between the seas) is meant to be understood as Jerusalem, then the second part of the verse (about being *in* or *facing* the holy mountain) gives further clarification as to where, specifically, in Jerusalem Antichrist will set up his headquarters. In other words, the two parts of this verse actually work together to give very specific information about the location of the headquarters of the Antichrist.

ISV: “When he pitches his royal pavilions between the seas facing the mountain of holy Glory…”.

NET: “He will pitch his royal tents between the seas toward the beautiful holy mountain…”.

KJV: “And he shall plant the tabernacles of his palace between the seas in the glorious holy mountain…”.

This makes contextual sense as well, because this setting up of the palace tents occurs just before the Antichrist enters the temple and declares himself to be God. We can tell this by seeing that verse Daniel 11:45 is connected to 12:1, a fact often overlooked because of the chapter break. This means that Antichrist is in exactly the right place at exactly the right time. He sets up his palace tents at the Temple Mount just before he enters the temple to declare himself God.

The latter part of this verse describes the Antichrist being killed. But again, because of the chronological connection to Daniel 12:1—which describes the beginning of a great persecution, using the same language Jesus used in Matthew 24 when talking about the persecution of the Antichrist after the abomination of desolation—we can surmise that this is the point when the Antichrist is killed, only to be resurrected again (the head wound that was healed in Revelation 13). We will discuss this exact moment in detail in later chapters, because I believe this point, just after the wars of Antichrist, when he is killed and resurrected, is directly linked to modern Jewish expectation of the so-called "Messiah ben Joseph," and is crucial to understanding how the Antichrist will deceive people at this time.

But for now, I only hope to make the point that if the Antichrist is said to make his capital in Jerusalem, in view of the Temple Mount, right after destroying the enemies of Israel, then it is strong support for the idea that the Antichrist is here attempting to fulfill two of the most important Jewish Messianic expectations: namely, that, at his strongest, when the whole world has been conquered by him, he makes Jerusalem the capital city of the world. This would seem to be fulfilling the non-negotiable expectation that Jerusalem will be the capital city of the world in Messianic times (Isaiah 2:1–4) as well as the belief that the Messiah will be ruling from the very temple itself (Isaiah 18:7). In other words, the Antichrist will be trying to fake the millennial reign of Christ (a point we will discuss in great detail in later chapters).

2 Thessalonians 2:4

> Who opposes and exalts himself above all that is called God or that is worshiped, so that he sits as God in the

> temple of God, showing himself that he is God. (2 Thessalonians 2:4)

The Antichrist sitting in the temple and declaring himself to be higher than God is mentioned in several places in Scripture (see Matthew 24:15 and Daniel 8:11). This gives us circumstantial evidence that supports the thesis that the Antichrist will claim to be the Messiah.

The rebuilding of the temple in Jerusalem is obviously a prerequisite for this event. (However, it should be noted that a more simple structure like a tabernacle would suffice, as the Greek word Paul uses in 2 Thessalonians 2:4 is *naos,* referring to the sanctuary, not necessarily the temple—though it could be the sanctuary in a rebuilt temple. For simplicity, as well as because I think it is the most likely option, I will refer to the structure as a "temple."). A rebuilt temple and the restarting of the sacrificial system in Jerusalem are very important parts of messianic expectations for the Jews, who believe that one of the two main ways to tell whether a person is really the Messiah is whether the temple system is revived by him.[14]

In addition, rebuilding such a structure on the Temple Mount, which is currently occupied by one of the holiest sites in Islam, the Dome of the Rock, would almost inevitably start a major war with the Muslim nations that surround Israel. I will suggest in detail later that Islamic eschatology dictates that all Muslims fight this particular war, which they believe will be preceded by a man

---

[14] "For our Talmudic sages ["Messianic redemption"], was the fulfillment of the exalted oracles of our biblical prophets and the revival of the Temple in Jerusalem."—Glickman, Rabbi Elaine Rose (2013-02-21). *The Messiah and the Jews: Three Thousand Years of Tradition, Belief and Hope* (Kindle Locations 622-623). Jewish Lights Publishing. Kindle Edition.

claiming to be the Jewish Messiah and the location of the Ark of the Covenant.

Once that war is initiated, it will cause the other main event Jews believe must happen for a man to validate his messianic claims: fight an epic war with the enemies of Israel and be victorious over them. In other words, the rebuilding of the temple sets the stage for the Antichrist to validate his Messianic claims to the Jews and everyone else. I will discuss this in detail in chapter 3, "The Wars of Antichrist."

It's important to take a step back and consider that the mere idea of the Antichrist sitting in a Jewish temple presupposes him giving a kind of legitimacy to the Jewish religion. When he does this, the temple will be "defiled" and the daily sacrifices that apparently will have been going on for some time will stop.[15] The fact that the daily sacrifices are stopped at this point is often used to promote the idea that the Antichrist will sit in the temple simply for the purpose of blaspheming Yahweh and disrespecting the temple, as if to say to everyone that the Jewish religion is untrue. I would take exception to this idea and suggest another interpretation of the so-called abomination of desolation.

The Abomination of Desolation

The abomination of desolation, the event that occurs in the middle of the seventieth week of Daniel, will indeed be the height of blasphemy, because the Antichrist's exaltation of himself as God is untrue. It was not blasphemy for Jesus to claim to be divine, as the Pharisees believed, because He was, in fact, God. However, it will be blasphemy and an abomination when the Antichrist makes

---

[15] Daniel 12:11.

the same claim. I suggest that the defiling of the temple occurs not because the Antichrist is claiming that God is bad or presenting any other type of overt, verbal blasphemy, but because he claims to be God.

This event and related Scriptures show that the Antichrist is actually carrying his Messianic theology of the first three and a half years to its logical conclusion with the abomination of desolation. He would not ostensibly be disrespecting the Jewish religion; he would be attempting to be seen as fulfilling it.

What I mean is that the two main actions that Antichrist takes at the abomination event are in line with Christian theology. Christians agree that the Messiah is also God and that animal sacrifices should be stopped when the Messiah comes. This is standard Christian theology that can be demonstrated from the Scriptures. In fact, there is even a Jewish rabbinic tradition stating that when Messiah comes, sacrifices will cease.[16] In addition, even though a modern Jew would argue passionately that the Messiah, when He comes, will not be God but rather only a man, he could no doubt be convinced of his error on this point by the same Old Testament Scriptures that Christian evangelists use to convince Jewish people that the real Messiah, Jesus, was in fact God and sacrifices should cease. This would especially be true if the person showing the Jews those Scriptures was also able to raise the dead and call down fire from heaven as the False Prophet will be able to do.

---

[16] According to Leviticus Rabbah 9:7 and Pesiqta Rabbati 12, several ancient rabbis taught the following: "*In the Age to Come all sacrifices will cease, but the thank offering will never cease*; all songs will cease, but the songs of thanksgiving will never cease." (Cited in Hartmut Gese, *Essays in Biblical Theology* 133).

I submit the possibility that what the church father Ambrose said is true: “Antichrist will attempt to prove from scripture that he is the Christ.”

Further evidence that the Antichrist is actually reinforcing his claim to be the Messiah with the abomination event can be seen by the two other actions he takes at that point. Revelation 13:14–15 states that the Antichrist sets up an image of himself. We know from other passages in Scripture that this image will be set up in the temple.[17] The people of the world will apparently be forced to worship this image under penalty of death. The institution of this necessarily involves a worldwide or semi-worldwide pilgrimage to Jerusalem; if people are supposed to choose between worshipping the image or being killed by it, they must, it would seem, be physically present to do so. I would also argue that at least one way of worshipping will be the offering of gold, silver, and precious stones (Daniel 11:38 and Revelation 18:12, to be discussed in later chapters), which further suggests that people who worship the Antichrist must go to Jerusalem to do so.

I contend that the reason the Antichrist sets an image of himself in the temple is related to his messianic claims. He is trying to make it look like he is fulfilling a very important prophecy about the true Messiah.

Isaiah 60:3–22 and 18:7 and Zechariah 14:16–18 say that when the Messiah comes, he will rule the world from the temple and cause all the nations to make a pilgrimage to Jerusalem to offer praise and worship. The problem the Antichrist will face in attempting to falsify this prophecy is logistics. He is not able or willing to sit in the temple to receive worship for extended periods of time; he

---

[17] Daniel:12:11, 11:31; Matthew: 24:15.

apparently has other things to do, based on what Scripture says about his career after this event. So the image he sets up is a kind of stand-in for him. He gets to have all the legitimacy of seemingly fulfilling one of the most important aspects of messianic prophecies, while not actually having to be physically present at the temple.

This also argues against the aforementioned belief that the abomination event is somehow an attempt to distance himself from Judaism. If all the people are forced to go to a Jewish temple to worship him, it can be reasonably assumed that he is forcing people to conform to Judaism in some way.

Fleeing Judah?

Something else that happens at the abomination event that seems to support the idea that the Antichrist is bolstering his Messianic claim and not diminishing it is the persecution that begins at that exact time. Apparently, not everyone in Israel will see the abomination as blasphemy at all; in fact, many will see his declaration to be God as scriptural truth.

Jesus said in Matthew 24:15–21 that the abomination will spark the greatest persecution the world will ever see, and that it is of the utmost importance for people to leave Jerusalem very quickly when they see it occur if they want to escape the persecution.

We can assume that many who believe the Antichrist's claim to be God will be the people who do the actual persecuting. The Antichrist apparently will tell everyone that it will then be time to do away with those who are not on board with his program. Though it goes without saying that many Gentiles will be a part of the group of people who worship the Antichrist, we seem to forget that the Bible implies that the vast majority of Jews will, too.

Zechariah 13:8–9 says that only one-third of national Israel will repent in the end times. Therefore, it can be reasonably argued that many of them will, like many of the Gentiles, worship the Antichrist. If almost two-thirds of the Jews in Jerusalem will worship the Antichrist, then this warning to flee Jerusalem at the point when the Antichrist demands worship can only mean that Jerusalem will have embraced the Antichrist in the vast majority. Apparently, there will be enough adherents to the Antichrist's theology that those who don't follow it must leave Jerusalem if they want to save their lives.

In conclusion, the idea that the Antichrist will claim to be the Messiah is supported by everything we know about the abomination of desolation, including: the Antichrist's declaration of himself as God after a major victory over the enemies of Israel; the stopping of the daily sacrifices; the setting up of an image to be worshipped by the world; and the great persecution that has its epicenter in Judea.

Inconclusive Proof Texts

I will now show two examples of verses used by the church fathers to bolster their case that the Antichrist will claim to be the Jewish Messiah that I believe are inconclusive, and therefore do not use when arguing this case. I am spending time on these verses because I believe those who use these verses to support this view are doing so irresponsibly and draw unnecessary criticism to the hypothesis when doing so. However, for our purposes, discussing these verses is profitable because it brings up some interesting points that that should be addressed.

Genesis 49:17

As we have already seen, many of the church fathers believed that the Antichrist would come from the tribe of Dan. The verse often used to support this belief is found in Genesis 49, which describes Jacob gathering his sons around him before his death in order to "tell [them] what shall befall [them] in the last days."

When Jacob comes to Dan, he says: "Dan shall be a serpent by the way, A viper by the path, That bites the horse's heels So that its rider shall fall backward" (Genesis 49:17).

Some assert that this verse points to the Antichrist by linking it to Genesis 3:15, which describes the curse given to the serpent in the Garden of Eden: "And I will put enmity Between you and the woman, And between your seed and her Seed; He shall bruise your head, And you shall bruise His heel."

However, I am not convinced that a clear case can be made for linking these two verses, if for no other reason than the fact that the serpent biting the heel of a horse, causing the rider to fall backwards (Genesis 49) seems distinctly different from the serpent bruising the heel of the seed of the woman (Genesis 3). The seed of the woman is widely understood to be Jesus Christ.

Genesis 49:17 is an interesting verse, especially in light of the "last-days" remark in 49:1. There are also other interesting prophecies about Dan, such as in Deuteronomy 33:22, which may ultimately be shown to be related to the Antichrist. However, some of the early church fathers might have been too overeager in their attempts to apply Genesis 49:17 to the Antichrist; I feel it would be irresponsible to be dogmatic about the view that the Antichrist will come from the tribe of Dan. I suppose I wouldn't be surprised if the Antichrist came from the tribe of Dan, as it is, so far as I can tell, a possibility, but I don't think that one can make a clear enough case from the Scriptures to call it a likelihood.

There are many interesting things to discuss regarding the topic of the lineage of the Antichrist, so, before we move on to the next verse, I want to take some time to explore this issue.

From the Line of David

Jewish expectations are that the Messiah will be from the line of David (who was of the tribe of Judah). The *Encyclopedia Judaica* says that "the rabbis agree he is of Davidic lineage (based on Hos. 3:5 and Jer. 30:9)."[18] The *Jewish Encyclopedia* adds that being from the Davidic line is "essential to the Messianic mission,"[19] and asserts that the reports that the Messianic pretender of the second century, Bar Kokhba, was from the Davidic line.

An example of how non-negotiable this idea that the Messiah will be from the line of David is to the Jewish people can be demonstrated in the attempts of historic false messiahs to at least claim to be from the line of David. We have already mentioned Bar Kokhba, but Sabbatai Zevi, the widely accepted false messiah of the seventeenth century AD, also claimed to be of the Davidic line,[20] though he offered no proof of the claim.

---

[18] Jewish Virtual Library. *Messiah*, 2008. http://www.jewishvirtuallibrary.org/jsource/judaica/ejud_0002_0014_0_13744.html.

[19] "Bar Kokba and Bar Kokba War" *Jewish Encyclopedia*, 1906. http://www.jewishencyclopedia.com/articles/2471-bar-kokba-and-bar-kokba-war.

[20] Joseph Kastein. *The Messiah of Ismir: Sabbatai Zevi*. Viking Press, n.d., http://archive.org/stream/MN41362ucmf_0/MN41362ucmf_0_djvu.txt.

It is difficult to overemphasize how ingrained this idea is in Judaism, and it seems unlikely, therefore, that the Antichrist could make any claim to be the Messiah without some evidence that he was of the Davidic line.

It is interesting that, due to historic circumstances, most Jews today have no way of telling which tribe they are from. The possible exceptions to this are the tribes of Levi and Judah. Those claiming to be of the tribe of Levi (the priest class that often features the last name "Cohen") historically have had very restrictive rules concerning marrying within the tribe. This has led to a unique opportunity for genetic research that has demonstrated quite conclusively a very specific genetic distinction among those claiming to be descended from Levi. The distinction has come to be known in genetic research as "Y-chromosomal Aaron."

Proof of lineage within the tribe of Judah is less about genetic research and more about an argument from history. The ten northern tribes were conquered and scattered by the Assyrians before the Babylonians conquered the Southern Kingdom. It was primarily Judah and Dan that were taken captive and exiled to Babylon (Dan was more or less absorbed into the Southern Kingdom prior to the Babylonian exile). Since modern Judaism is derived from the Babylonian exiles, the case might be made that all modern Jews, in a sense, derive from Judah and Dan. However, this claim is rather difficult to substantiate, because, in many places, Scripture notes that representative communities from most of the other tribes resided in Judah before and after the exile.[21]

Despite this, the more important factor with regard to making a messianic claim seem genuine is proving that one is from the line

---

[21] Chuck Missler. "Mystery of the Myth: The Ten Lost Tribes", n.d. http://www.khouse.org/articles/1995/40/ .

of David. Many people have claimed to be descendants of David, offering various proofs. However, David Einsiedler from the Jewish Geological Society, after reviewing the best evidence for these claims in an excellent article entited "Can We Prove Descent from King David?" concludes:

> All we need is good evidence and records that go back that far and give convincing proof of our claim. So far, available records cannot do it. Some individuals rely on tradition and faith to back their claim. More power to them. The rest of us may have to wait for that promised descendant—the Messiah.[22]

This is an interesting remark expressing the Jewish belief that when the Messiah comes, He will reveal information about the tribes of Israel. Many Jews believe it will actually be the prophet Elijah who will somehow reveal information about the genealogy of the Messiah, proving Him to be from the line of David.

One final point of interest regarding the end-times tribal awareness of at least certain Jews concerns the enigmatic 144,000 Jews who are sealed by God during the Day of the Lord judgments. We know from Revelation 7:4–8 that these Jews will be chosen from each of the twelve tribes of Israel—with the possible exception of Dan, who is not mentioned.

> And I heard the number of those who were sealed. One hundred and forty-four thousand of all the tribes of the children of Israel were sealed: of the tribe of Judah twelve thousand were sealed; of the tribe of Reuben twelve thousand were sealed; of the tribe of Gad twelve thousand

---

[22] David Einsiedler. "Can We Prove Descent from King David?" *Avotaynu: The International Review of Jewish Genealogy,* Vol. VIII No. 3 (1992): 29.

> were sealed; of the tribe of Asher twelve thousand were sealed; of the tribe of Naphtali twelve thousand were sealed; of the tribe of Manasseh twelve thousand were sealed; of the tribe of Simeon twelve thousand were sealed; of the tribe of Levi twelve thousand were sealed; of the tribe of Issachar twelve thousand were sealed; of the tribe of Zebulun twelve thousand were sealed; of the tribe of Joseph twelve thousand were sealed; of the tribe of Benjamin twelve thousand were sealed. (Revelation 7:4–8)

Somehow, the tribal identity of at least these Jews is known at this point. It could be that these men did not know their tribal identity before they were sealed. In other words, perhaps only God knew which tribe these men were from. This is very possible, and I tend to lean toward that conclusion. However, it could also be that Jewish tribal identity will somehow be common knowledge in the last days. This seems logical, because if the temple sacrifices are instituted again, as they will be in the first half of Daniel's seventieth week, at least the members of the tribe of Levi would have to be identified in order for them to function as priests. This could happen quite easily through a combination of certain records being discovered and genetic research, as Einsiedler was quoted earlier as saying.

> I don't want to make any firm conclusion on this point about the 144,000, as I'm not sure that we can, based on Scripture. I only submit that Jewish tribal knowledge will once again be understood in the time of the 144,000 and in the Millennium.[23] Whether that knowledge comes to light before the 144,000 are sealed is an open question, but if it

[23] Ezekiel 48: 1–35.

does, then it would be very easy for the Antichrist to prove his tribal identity, whatever it may be.

Ezekiel 28:10

> "You shall die the death of the uncircumcised by the hand of aliens; For I have spoken," says the Lord GOD. (Ezekiel 28:10)

This verse is often used to prove that the Antichrist will be Jewish; there are some pros and cons for accepting that idea.

First, we need to understand the context. Ezekiel 28 is often grouped with Isaiah 14, because both passages share a similar pattern. They begin with a proclamation of the impending judgment of an earthly king: the king of Babylon in the case of Isaiah and the king of Tyre in Ezekiel. In both passages, it becomes apparent that this also should be taken as a prophecy of the future judgment of Satan himself.

In Ezekiel 28, phrases like "you were in Eden, the garden of God" and "you were the anointed cherub who covers; I established you; You were on the holy mountain of God" seem to go beyond the scope of anything that could, even allegorically, be explained only by having the king of Tyre in view. Similar phrases like "how you are fallen from heaven, O Lucifer, son of the morning" and others force a similar conclusion in Isaiah 14. In almost every case in these two passages, the same phrases that cannot be attributed to the earthly kings also happened to be aspects of either Satan or the Antichrist in other places in Scripture.

In both of these passages, Satan as well as the Antichrist is in view. This is probably because, when proclaiming the defeat of Satan by God, it is appropriate to include a discussion of the

Antichrist's defeat—because the Antichrist seems to be the primary agent through which Satan attempts his end-times coup. In Ezekiel 28, the idea that the Antichrist is in view seems likely by the use of phrases like that found in verse 2, which says: "Because your heart is lifted up, And you say, 'I am a god, I sit in the seat of god'" (see also 28:6 and 28:9). This corresponds to the Antichrist claiming to be God and sitting in the temple of God (2 Thessalonians 2:4; Isaiah 14:13; Matthew 24:15; Daniel 8:9–11, 11:36).

This brings us to verse 10, which says: "You shall die the death of the uncircumcised by the hand of aliens." This verse is used to argue that the person in view must be a circumcised (Jewish) person if he was being threatened with being killed as an uncircumcised person is killed. The addition of "by the hand of aliens" seems to add further weight to this argument.

While I find this interpretation to be a genuine possibility, partly because it appears in such an interesting context, I am wary of endorsing it. Although the term "death of the uncircumcised" only appears here in Scripture, and is therefore difficult to analyze, the general idea seems to be a prominent one four chapters later in Ezekiel 32, where the Egyptian Pharaoh is told that he will die in the "midst of the circumcised." Additionally, the phrase, "by the hand of aliens," elsewhere in Ezekiel refers to the Babylonians. In both cases, it is clear that the person being spoken to is not Jewish.

Even though I lean toward dismissing this verse, the reason I'm not too quick to do so is that, after careful study of all of the occasions in which similar phrases are used in Ezekiel, I am convinced that the various proclamations of judgments on these specific nations have aspects that demand an eschatological fulfillment for them to be completely fulfilled. In other words, the nations involved in this series of judgments in Ezekiel where we find this "uncircumcised" motif will not be completely judged until the end times. Therefore, I'm not sure if the references are literal, given the possibility that in the end times, the Antichrist might actually force all nations that serve him to be circumcised. That would not just be in line with the Jewish view that in the end times all nations will be monotheistic servants of Yahweh, but it would also be in line with the apparent pilgrimage to the temple the Antichrist institutes.

In conclusion, I will not add my voice to those claiming dogmatically that Ezekiel 28:10 is a reference to a Jewish Antichrist. However, I think that this section of Scripture is very interesting, especially because it seems clear that the Antichrist is in view. In addition, this series of prophecies in Ezekiel must be seen as a double fulfillment, with the completion of the judgments occurring in an eschatological context. Therefore, I do think this verse may give support to the Jewish Antichrist theory, even if not in the usual way suggested.

Chapter 3

The Wars of Antichrist

One of the clearest doctrines of the Antichrist is that he is a man of war. He seems to come on the scene by conquering a number of countries that surround Israel (Daniel 11:40–45). One of the things the people who worship the Antichrist in Revelation 13 are so impressed with about him is his ability to defeat his enemies in war: "They worshiped the beast, saying, 'Who is like the beast? Who is able to make war with him?'" (Revelation 13:4b).

We're told in Daniel 11:38–39 that the Antichrist's war-making capability is empowered by his worship of a "god of fortresses," which I believe is a reference to Satan, because Revelation 13:2 and 4 state directly that it is the "dragon" (a clear reference to Satan) who gives the Antichrist his power to subdue the nations with war. Regardless of who, exactly, this "god of fortresses" is that the Antichrist uses to help with his military victories, the fact that he has such supernatural military victories is evident.

The Lord also tells us in Matthew 24 that, just preceding the abomination of desolation event, which occurs at the midpoint of the seventieth week, there will be "wars and rumors of wars." In addition, the first seal (Revelation 6:1–2) describes the Antichrist going out "conquering and to conquer."

The last few verses of Daniel chapter 11 name the very kings the Antichrist will defeat, as well provide a great many other details that I believe lead us to the undeniable conclusion that the

Antichrist is attempting to fulfill one of the most, if not the most, important prophecies of the Jewish Messiah: that he must conquer the enemies of Israel.

Daniel 11:40 is the first verse in this section about the wars of Antichrist:

> At the time of the end the king of the South shall attack him; and the king of the North shall come against him like a whirlwind, with chariots, horsemen, and with many ships; and he shall enter the countries, overwhelm them, and pass through.

The "king of the south" is a reference to Israel's historic enemy, Egypt, and has been used to refer to Egypt throughout the first part of this chapter. This point is not contested by many; in fact, the word "Egypt" even appears explicitly twice, a few verses later, in a passage that speaks of the subjection of Egypt to the Antichrist:

> He shall stretch out his hand against the countries, and the land of Egypt shall not escape. He shall have power over the treasures of gold and silver, and over all the precious things of Egypt; also the Libyans and Ethiopians shall follow at his heels. (Daniel 11:42–43)

It is interesting to see that Egypt attacks the Antichrist first (verse 40). And, even though Antichrist completely subdues Egypt, that nation's aggression toward him is worthy of noting, and will be important when we study Islamic eschatology in later chapters.

Conservative expositors and scholars debate the identity of the "king of the north," another conquest of the Antichrist (verse 40). During the Cold War, it was proposed that the king of the north was Russia. However, that view seems to have been based more on the geopolitics of the day rather than on any clue from the text itself. These days, it is generally accepted that the king of the north represents the same thing it has throughout the earlier portion of the chapter, which includes parts of modern-day Iran, Iraq, Turkey, Syria, Afghanistan, and a few others. For more on this, I recommend the excellent paper by Dr. J. Paul Tanner, "Daniel's 'King of the North': Do We Owe Russia an Apology?"[24] Dr. Tanner concludes his paper this way:

> To be hermeneutically consistent, the "king of the North" ought to be interpreted in light of the meaning the phrase has had throughout the chapter.... I would like to submit that the "King of the North" is a confederation of northern Arab nations that will attack the Antichrist and his forces in this military conflict centered in the Middle East.[25]

So, to sum up the first part of this passage, the Antichrist is attacked by Egypt and a northern coalition of Arab states. But, even though he is attacked first, he completely crushes these historic enemies of Israel, subdues them, and takes their resources.

A quick word on the idea that these are the "historic" enemies of Israel: Not only are these two groups (Egypt and this cluster of Arab countries) consistently "bad guys" in the Bible, they also are specifically said to be destroyed and subdued by the Messiah during the Messianic Age (Isaiah 11:16, 19:23–25, and 27:12–13; Micah 7:12; Zechariah 14:18–19). This suggests that the Antichrist is attempting to fulfill these prophecies. At the very least, it would be very tempting for a Jewish person to believe that the person who finally destroys their incredibly antagonistic neighbors and

---

[24] J. Paul Tanner, "Daniel's 'King of the North': Do We Owe Russia an Apology?," JETS 35 (1992):315–28.
[25] Ibid.

forces them to capitulate to Israel is at least a strong candidate for the Messiah.

Why isn't the fact that the Antichrist will destroy and subdue the enemies of Israel talked about more in modern prophecy teaching? The answer is that it doesn't fit with most of the modern views of the Antichrist. Why would the Antichrist—who, they think, is either a man of peace or a Muslim—destroy the Muslim world? It doesn't fit with many of the mainstream views, so almost no one dwells on this passage.

The Antichrist Enters the Glorious Land

The next part of this prophecy gives even further proof that the Antichrist is knowingly attempting to root out all the enemies of Israel and fulfill specific prophecies about the Messiah (though many people view the next few verses in exactly the opposite way): "He shall also enter the Glorious Land, and many countries shall be overthrown; but these shall escape from his hand: Edom, Moab, and the prominent people of Ammon" (Daniel 11:41).

Most commentaries I have read interpret this to mean that after the Antichrist conquers Egypt and the other Arab countries, he enters Israel to attack the Jews as well. However, not only does nothing in this text suggest that he is attacking Jewish countries, but I believe the verse explicitly says the exact opposite is happening. This verse indicates that the Antichrist is entering Israel not to conquer the Jews, but the parts of Israel that are held by Israel's enemies. In other words, after the Antichrist's macro conquests of the main enemies of Israel (Egypt, Iran, etc.), he then enters Israel to mop up the micro enemies of Israel that are their immediate neighbors, like the Palestinians.

This is most evident by the fact that the three places mentioned in verse 41, Edom, Moab, and Ammon (all of which are Arab nations today), "escape" from the Antichrist's hands. The only reason to describe these enemies as "escaping" is to show that they were being pursued by the Antichrist in the first place. These groups, too, are consistently mentioned as being conquered in the Messianic Age. Also note that the passage says that Antichrist enters the Glorious Land and overthrows "many countries"—a phrase that certainly makes sense if he is attacking other non-Jewish countries in and around Israel like Edom, Moab and Ammon.

Modern Israel holds a very small portion of the land as defined in Genesis 15:18–21, or the land conquered by King David (see map). It is of the utmost importance to realize that several prophecies in Scripture say when the Messiah comes, He will conquer the whole land of Israel—including, for example, the coastlands that are currently Palestinian-controlled (such as Gaza).

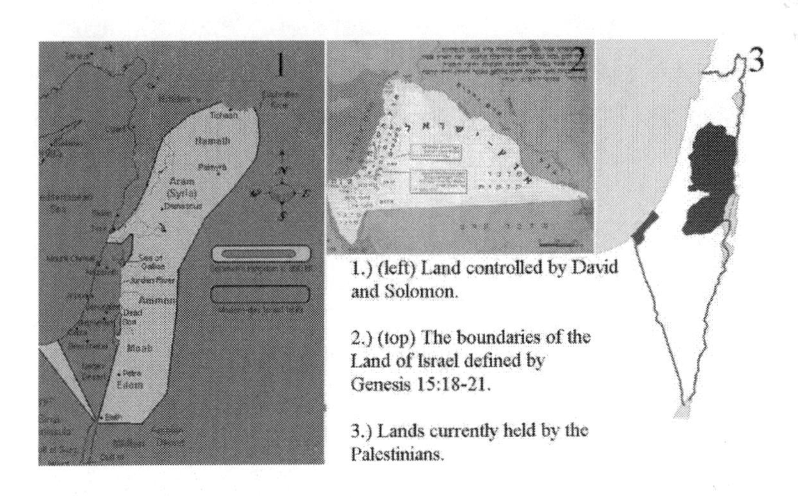

1.) (left) Land controlled by David and Solomon.

2.) (top) The boundaries of the Land of Israel defined by Genesis 15:18-21.

3.) Lands currently held by the Palestinians.

Zephaniah 2 describes how the real Messiah will take back lands from the micro enemies of Israel (in addition to the macro enemies mentioned in other places) during the Kingdom Age:

> For Gaza shall be forsaken, And Ashkelon desolate; They shall drive out Ashdod at noonday, And Ekron shall be uprooted. Woe to the inhabitants of the seacoast, The nation of the Cherethites! The word of the LORD is against you, O Canaan, land of the Philistines: "I will destroy you; So there shall be no inhabitant." The seacoast shall be pastures, with shelters for shepherds and folds for flocks. The coast shall be for the remnant of the house of Judah; They shall feed their flocks there; In the houses of Ashkelon they shall lie down at evening. For the LORD their God will intervene for them, And return their captives.
>
> "I have heard the reproach of Moab, And the insults of the people of Ammon, With which they have reproached My people, And made arrogant threats against their borders. Therefore, as I live," Says the LORD of hosts, the God of Israel, "Surely Moab shall be like Sodom, And the people of Ammon like Gomorrah—Overrun with weeds and saltpits, And a perpetual desolation. The residue of My people shall plunder them, And the remnant of My people shall possess them." (Zephaniah 2:4–9)

I am proposing that the Antichrist will succeed in trying to fulfill much of this prophecy according to Daniel 11:41. He will indeed conquer Gaza, Ashdod, Ekron, and the coastlands, etc., and expand the borders of Israel; however, he fails in securing the others specifically named in Zephaniah 2 (Edom, Moab, and Ammon). These are in modern-day Jordan though they were a part of Israel during the reign of David.

This passage then functions as a help to those who will try to prove that the man everyone thinks is the Messiah (the Antichrist) isn't really the Messiah, because even though he almost fulfilled the Zephaniah 2 prophecy, he isn't able to totally do it; he lets some very important countries "escape from his hands." Nevertheless, what he does next is so astonishing that I doubt people will dwell on this failure for very long.

The Post-War Resurrection of the Antichrist

The next two verses in Daniel 11 that we have been studying are extremely important. Their significance has often been overlooked due to an unnecessary chapter break between Daniel 11:45, the last verse in the chapter, and Daniel 12:1:

> **Daniel 11:45:**And he shall plant the tents of his palace between the seas and the glorious holy mountain; yet he shall come to his end, and no one will help him.
>
> **Daniel 12:1: At that time** Michael shall stand up, The great prince who stands watch over the sons of your people; And there shall be **a time of trouble, Such as never was since there was a nation, Even to that time.** And at that time your people shall be delivered, Every one who is found written in the book. (emphasis added)

In chapter 2, I alluded to my belief that these two verses show that the Antichrist "coming to his end" must refer to his dying as a result of the "mortal head wound" mentioned in several places (see Revelation 13:3, 12, and 14) from which he eventually recovers in what seems to be a miraculous resurrection. In other words, I don't believe that the mention of the Antichrist coming to his end in Daniel 11:45 is speaking of his final end at all. I stated that one of the reasons for believing this is that the next verse, Daniel 12:1, starts with the words, "At that time," which chronologically connects the following events to the previous verse. Daniel 12:1 continues by saying: "At that time Michael shall stand up, The great prince who stands *watch* over the sons of your people; And there shall be a time of trouble, Such as never was since there was a nation, *Even* to that time…"

This means the Antichrist coming to his end just after his conquest of the enemies of Israel is directly followed by Michael "standing up" and the beginning of "a time of trouble, Such as never was since there was a nation, Even to that time."

I will include a footnote[26] explaining my belief about the significance of Michael "standing up" here and how it relates to the abomination of desolation and the so-called "time of trouble." But I believe a much more obvious connection to this event can be seen by the use of the phrase "a time of trouble, Such as never was since there was a nation, Even to that time." The Lord referenced this exact phrase in the Olivet Discourse, when He warned of the persecution that would follow the abomination of desolation (when the Antichrist declares himself to be God in the temple). He said the following in Matthew 24:

> Therefore when you see the "ABOMINATION of DESOLATION" spoken of by Daniel the prophet, standing in the holy place (whoever reads, let him understand), then let those who are in Judea flee to the mountains…. For then there will be great tribulation, **such as has not been since**

---

[26] Some people say that this is Michael standing up to protect his people. But, if that's the case, he kind of does a terrible job of it. Because, the minute he "stands up," there is **a time of trouble, Such as never was since there was a nation, Even to that time.** We find out from Zechariah 13 that starting at this very time, two-thirds of Israel, whom he is supposed to be protecting, are killed. It actually appears as though Michael stands up in order to let the destruction happen at the abomination of desolation.

> **the beginning of the world until this time, no, nor ever shall be. (**Matthew 24:15, 16, and 21, emphasis added)

Since we know that the abomination of desolation occurs at the midpoint of the seventieth week of Daniel, then we can piece together that the Antichrist, after defeating the enemies of Israel, is killed in Israel just before the midpoint. We can then infer that this killing of the Antichrist is not the end of the Antichrist, because he still has three and a half more years of destruction to complete. So, it must be that this is a reference to his being killed and yet seemingly coming back from the dead (Revelation 13:3, 12, and 14), and that this resurrection precedes his declaring himself to be God in the temple and the persecution or time of trouble that follows.

This theory about the timing of the Antichrist's wars, resurrection, and abomination of desolation has a very interesting connection to a Jewish eschatological belief that is almost completely unknown to evangelicals but might prove to be the most important false prophecy ever spoken, as it could be the main reason the Jews will embrace the Antichrist as their Messiah in the last days.

The Messiah ben Joseph Connection

You might be surprised to know that many Jewish people are waiting for a man to do exactly the things I just said the Antichrist will do. Namely, they are waiting for a man called Messiah ben Joseph to destroy the enemies of Israel and after these wars march victoriously to Israel, where he will be killed by his enemies, but then miraculously resurrected. His resurrection will be the beginning of the Messianic Age, but not before a rooting out and killing of those who will not submit to the new Messianic authority. If you are following me so far, you can see how scary this idea about Messiah ben Joseph is, because it essentially means the Jews are waiting on someone Christians know of as the Antichrist.

Let me first explain the concept of Messiah ben Joseph. The Talmud, one of the most important Jewish texts, when trying to reconcile the various natures of the Messiah in the Bible (suffering servant, king, and conqueror), came up with the idea that there will actually be two Messiahs in the end times. The first, Messiah ben Joseph, will precede Messiah ben David. Messiah ben David is considered to be the superior Messiah. Messiah ben Joseph will do all the things I just mentioned, and then Messiah ben David will be the one who actually rules over the Messianic Age as king.

There are many different views about how the end times will play out in the Jewish world, but this view about the two Messiahs is widely accepted by any Jew taking a literal view of the end times, probably because the concept of Messiah ben Joseph appears in the all-important Talmud, it was adopted and expanded on by almost every Jewish commentator in the Middle Ages, and has become a very entrenched belief in Judaism.

The following is what *the Jewish Encyclopedia* says about Messiah ben Joseph (follow the footnotes if you are interested in finding some of the sources for the beliefs about this).

> Messiah b. Joseph will appear prior to the coming of Messiah b. David; he will gather the children of Israel around him, march to Jerusalem, and there, after overcoming the hostile powers, reestablish the Temple-worship and set up his own dominion. Thereupon Armilus, according to one group of sources, or Gog and Magog, according to the other, will appear with their hosts before Jerusalem, wage war against Messiah b. Joseph, and slay

> him. His corpse, according to one group, will lie unburied in the streets of Jerusalem; according to the other, it will be hidden by the angels with the bodies of the Patriarchs, until Messiah b. David comes and resurrects him.[27]

This is so clearly a description of the Antichrist in Daniel 11 that prominent rabbis such as Isaac Abrabanel (1437–1508) have claimed that the Christians invented the concept of the Antichrist based on their view of Messiah ben Joseph.[28] This is an absurd assertion, but it helps show that even they see the obvious connection between a man they view as their savior and the man Christians call the Antichrist.

I should mention here that some modern Jewish believers are unaware of the concept of the two Messiahs, despite it being taught by almost every major sage since the Talmud. This is because there are numerous divergent beliefs about the Messiah in Judaism today. I have often had Jewish believers that say something like, "We don't believe that," respond with shock when I point to the teachings about Messiah ben Joseph in their favorite rabbis, like Rashi, Nahmanides, or Saadia. The point I will make later is that it isn't that important for modern Jewish people to have been taught these concepts in their modern synagogues; the important thing is that the teachings are there and they can be exploited by the Antichrist or the False Prophet when the time comes.

---

[27] "Messiah (Hebr., 'Ha-Mashiaḥ'; Aramaic, 'Meshiḥa' = 'Anointed One')." *Jewish Encyclopedia*, n.d. http://www.jewishencyclopedia.com/articles/10729-messiah#anchor16.

[28] Joseph Sarachek, D. H. L. "The Doctrine of the Messiah in Medieval Jewish Literature." 262–263. Jewish Theological Seminary of America, 1932.

The Extermination of Those Who Will Not Worship the Antichrist

For obvious reasons, the following doctrine held by many Jewish theologians hasn't been widely explained to non-Jews. But there is a belief that after the resurrection of Messiah ben Joseph, a time of cleansing of those who refuse to accept monotheism will be necessary in order to usher in the time of Messianic peace. Joseph Sarachek addresses this point in *The Doctrine of the Messiah in Medieval Jewish Literature:*

> **The general belief** is that when Israel becomes supreme, the unrepentant Gentiles and the inveterate foes among them will be extirpated ["to root out and destroy completely"[29]]. Others will accept monotheism. As a visible token of their acknowledgment they will practice some Jewish ordinances.[30] (emphasis added)

Sarachek is saying here that Jewish theologians generally believe that after Israel becomes supreme, those who won't accept Jewish monotheism will need to be found and completely wiped out. This sheds new light on why the greatest persecution of all time happens after the Antichrist officially declares his supremacy. It also explains why the epicenter of that persecution is in Judea and helps us to better understand the nature of the persecution and why it will be willingly carried out by so many.

In later chapters, we will more deeply explore Jewish eschatology, as well as Islamic eschatology, and see that they are both linked—

---

[29] http://www.merriam-webster.com/dictionary/extirpate.
[30] Joseph Sarachek. *The Doctrine of the Messiah in Medieval Jewish Literature,* p. 19.

and are, I believe, false doctrines that will play right into the hands of the Antichrist.

In this chapter, I have shown that the Antichrist is a man of war and that those whom he wars against are exclusively the enemies of Israel. I've made the case that this suggests he is defeating these enemies in order to look as if he is fulfilling the messianic prophecies I referenced. I stated that his death in verse 45 of Daniel 11 must be a reference to the mortal head wound that he will recover from, based on the following verse that links that period to the midpoint and the abomination of desolation. Finally, I've discussed the undeniable links to the Antichrist's actions in Daniel 11:40–45 and the Jewish belief in Messiah ben Joseph and how the persecution that Jesus and Daniel warned us about might be linked to the belief of the genocidal "cleansing" period after Messiah ben Joseph is resurrected.

Chapter 4

Mystery Babylon

An important section of Scripture that I believe strongly supports the thesis of this book can be found in Revelation 17–18, the chapters that talk about "Mystery Babylon." (I've written an entire book on this subject called *Mystery Babylon—When Jerusalem Embraces the Antichrist,* which I recommend to those who would like a more in-depth study on this topic.) In this chapter, I will do my best to hit some of the main points of "mystery Babylon," as well as discus some of the common objections to the theory that I am about to present.

Some very popular teachers assert that Mystery Babylon is metaphorical; in other words, it is not an actual city but symbolic of something else, possibly a worldwide pagan religious/financial system. They say this despite the fact that in Revelation 17:18, the angel, while interpreting John's vision, refers to the "woman" as a "city": "And the woman which thou sawest **is that great city**, which reigneth over the kings of the earth" (emphasis added).

Mystery Babylon is referred to as a "city" eight times in the book of Revelation, and many of the things that happen to it in the narrative seem to be talking about a literal city. For instance, the city is burned down and the smoke can be seen from the nearby sea; merchants sell items to it; and it experiences famine. These plus many other factors, we will soon see, cause many to believe that it is in fact a literal city, just as the angel said.

Those who see Mystery Babylon as a literal city have proposed several candidates for the identity of the city, including:

1. Rome or Vatican City. Many early reformers saw Mystery Babylon as Rome. Somewhat ironically, the Catholic Church, on the Vatican website, also teaches that it is Rome[31]—though it is referring to ancient pagan Rome, whereas the Protestant reformers would say that it was the Rome of the Catholic Church.

2. Babylon. Some suggest Mystery Babylon is the actual city of Babylon in Iraq. In this scenario, they say the city will be rebuilt in the future.

3. Mecca or some other Arab cities. This view has been especially popular recently.

4. Jerusalem. This is the view that will be defended in this chapter.

5. New York City, as well as a long list of other, less popular candidates.

I believe Mystery Babylon is the last-days city of Jerusalem. I choose my words very carefully in this description. In other words, it's not referring to any previous Jerusalem, or even to Jerusalem today; it is the Jerusalem of the end times, when the people of that city make the temporary mistake of accepting the Antichrist as Messiah and promote his worship to the rest of the world—the Jerusalem that becomes the capital city of the world under the Antichrist's authority.

---

[31] http://www.vatican.va/archive/ENG0839/_P12J.HTM.

We know that the Antichrist will choose Jerusalem as the place to declare himself to be God (2 Thessalonians 2:4; Matthew 24:15; and Daniel 11:31–32). And we know that the greatest religious persecution of all time, which is prompted by the abomination of desolation, will happen in the city of Jerusalem (Matthew 24:15–21), and that the Antichrist seems to set up his headquarters in the city itself (Daniel 11:45). So, we already understand that there is a relationship between the Antichrist and the city of Jerusalem in the last days. We have also seen the Antichrist is attempting to fulfill Messianic prophecies, and we know that the most important of those prophecies are things like setting up Jerusalem as the capital city of the world (Isaiah 2:1–4) as well as setting up a worldwide pilgrimage system enabling the Gentiles to flow into Jerusalem (Isaiah 60:3–22; Isaiah 18:7; Zechariah 14:16–18). We will see that these things are taking place in Mystery Babylon, and we will look at what I believe are scriptural proofs that the term refers to the last-days Jerusalem.

Basics of Mystery Babylon

Before we get into specifics, it will be helpful to go over some of the basics about what John saw in his vision about Mystery Babylon.

John saw a vision of a woman riding a seven-headed, ten-horned beast—the same beast seen earlier in Revelation 13, which is by this time an established reference to the Antichrist. As I mentioned, we are told specifically by an angelic interpreter in Revelation 17:18 that the woman is a city. So, the basic idea is that John saw a city riding the Antichrist. We know that the city is deceived, because she says she has found her husband and her king (Revelation 18:7). She is extremely happy with the beast she is riding at first, but she finds later on, at the very end, that the beast turns on her and tries to destroy the city (Revelation 17:16–17).

We also know that the city is responsible for the promotion of the Antichrist's worship to the rest of the world because of verses like Revelation 17:2b, which says: "The inhabitants of the earth were made drunk with the wine of **her fornication"** (emphasis added).

Or, as Revelation 18:3 puts it, "For all nations have drunk the wine of **the passion** of her [fornication]" (ESV, emphasis added).

The idea is that Mystery Babylon herself is so deceived by the Antichrist that she is passionately worshiping him as her long-awaited king and husband. So intense is the passion of her fornication that the entire world is drawn in (made drunk) and deceived into doing this with her.

Now, a few biblical reasons to validate this theory.

Blood of the Prophets

The last verse of Revelation 18 makes a very impressive statement: "And in her was found the blood of prophets and saints, and of all who were slain on the earth" (Revelation 18:24). I submit that the only city this can apply to is Jerusalem. Let's take each part separately to see why.

The idea that the blood of prophets was found in this city is interesting, because there is only one place that the prophets were ever killed in Scripture: Jerusalem. In fact, Jesus actually says that it is *impossible* for a prophet to be killed anywhere except Jerusalem!

> The same day there came certain of the Pharisees, saying unto him, "Get thee out, and depart hence: for Herod will kill thee." And he said unto them, "Go ye, and tell that fox, behold, I cast out devils, and I do cures today and tomorrow, and the third day I shall be perfected. Nevertheless I must walk today, and tomorrow, and the day following: **for it cannot be that a prophet perish out of Jerusalem."** (Luke 13:31–33, emphasis added)

He reiterates this point in the next verse: "O Jerusalem, Jerusalem, which killest the prophets" (Luke 13:34a).

That should end the discussion about which city is responsible for killing the prophets, but what do we make of the next part of the verse in Revelation 18:24, which says "the blood of **all who were slain on the earth"** is found in this city. (emphasis added). You might think we need to go looking for somewhere besides Jerusalem to find a place responsible for *all* the blood of the slain, but Jesus actually said that Jerusalem would be blamed for all the righteous blood shed on the earth, not just for the people who were killed there.

> Therefore, indeed, I send you prophets, wise men, and scribes: some of them you will kill and crucify, and some of them you will scourge in your synagogues and persecute from city to city, **that on you may come all the righteous blood shed on the earth, from the blood of righteous Abel to the blood of Zechariah**, son of Berechiah, whom you murdered between the temple and the altar. (Matthew 23:34–35, emphasis added)

No other city in Scripture is said to have this kind of blame put on it; therefore, passages like Revelation 18:24 about Mystery Babylon being blamed for the blood of the prophets, etc., must be intended to point directly to Jerusalem, because we have explicit references from the Lord Himself about this very issue.

Harlot

Take even the very idea of a city being a harlot: Jerusalem is specifically called a "harlot" hundreds of times in Scripture, and always in a spiritual context—the harlotry of following false gods and killing prophets. Just a small sampling of this can be found in Isaiah 1:21: "How is the faithful city become an harlot! It was full of judgment; righteousness lodged in it; but now murderers."

Ezekiel 16 is entirely about this subject, and it starts: "Again the word of the LORD came unto me, saying, Son of man, cause Jerusalem to know her abominations."

In fact, Ezekiel spends the whole chapter saying things like:

> But thou didst trust in thine own beauty, and playedst the harlot because of thy renown, and pouredst out thy fornications on every one that passed by; his it was. And of thy garments thou didst take, and deckedst thy high places with divers colours, and playedst the harlot thereupon: the like things shall not come, neither shall it be so." (Ezekiel 16:15–16)

Mystery Babylon is called the "Mother of Harlots." Some try to make this phrase more than the text makes of it. They see it requiring the city to be the source of all the world's evil from time immemorial, but that is not what I believe the text is intending. I believe this is talking about Jerusalem, which is at this point committing the worst kind of adultery (because she, of all cities, should know better than to be worshipping a false god like the Antichrist). Also, a consistent idiom in Scripture conveys the idea that cities have children, which are often referred to as "daughters," "sons," or simply "children." So "harlots," as in "mother of harlots," simply refers to Jerusalem's inhabitants. One example of the use of this concept can be seen when Jesus was on the road to be crucified:

> But Jesus turning unto them said, **Daughters of Jerusalem**, weep not for me, but weep for yourselves, and for your children. For, behold, the days are coming, in which they shall say, 'Blessed are the barren, and the wombs that never bare, and the paps which never gave suck.'" (Luke 23:28–29, emphasis added)

Isaiah 4:4, when speaking of the institution of the millennial kingdom, says:

> When the Lord has washed away the filth of the **daughters of Zion**, and purged the blood of Jerusalem from her midst, by the spirit of judgment and by the spirit of burning. (Isaiah 4:4, emphasis added)

Here is yet another example of the inhabitants of a city being referred to as "children" of that city:

> O Jerusalem, Jerusalem, the one who kills the prophets and stones those who are sent to her! How often I wanted to gather **your children** together, as a hen gathers her chicks under her wings, but you were not willing! See! Your house is left to you desolate. (Matthew 23:37–38, emphasis added)

Jerusalem is constantly warned in Scripture that if it does not turn from its harlotries, it will be judged. As we go through Revelation 17–18, we find that the specific judgments Mystery Babylon gets are the exact same as those promised to Jerusalem because of its spiritual harlotry. Jerusalem is judged in the end times for the purpose of ending this harlotry as a means of purification, and it's clear that this happens just before the Millennium. The following is just one example from Ezekiel 43 where Ezekiel is talking to God while looking at the millennial temple. God is talking about the things that will happen just before the temple He is showing Ezekiel will be able to be built:

> And he said to me, "Son of man, this is the place of my throne and the place of the soles of my feet, where I will dwell in the midst of the people of Israel forever. And the house of Israel shall no more defile my holy name, neither they, nor their kings, **by their whoring** and by the dead bodies of their kings at their high places, by setting their threshold by my threshold and their doorposts beside my doorposts, with only a wall between me and them. They have defiled my holy name by their abominations that they have committed, **so I have consumed them in my anger**. **Now let them put away their whoring** and the dead bodies of their kings far from me, and I will dwell in their midst forever." (Ezekiel 43:7–9, emphasis added)

The judgment of Jerusalem for the purpose of purification that occurs just before the Millennium is mentioned in several other places (Zechariah 14:1–5, 13:1–9; Revelation 16:18–21; Zephaniah 1:4–18).

Items Sold to Mystery Babylon

Most people who have different theories about Mystery Babylon have to view the twenty-nine items in Revelation 18 that are sold to Mystery Babylon by the merchants as symbolic (just an allegory of economic wealth). This is because the items listed are kind of odd and don't seem like things that any modern city would be purchasing in large quantities. But as I show in my book, each of the items brought to Mystery Babylon has some explicit use in the temple system, whether to do with offerings that are to be made at the temple or with building up the fake millennial Jerusalem. Why are the merchants getting so rich? Let's look at some of examples and I will show you.

The first items mentioned are "gold and silver, precious stones." The *only* other place this *exact phrase* is used is in describing the specific offerings needed to worship the Antichrist's god in Daniel 11: "But in their place he shall honor a god of fortresses; and a god which his fathers did not know he shall honor with **gold and silver, with precious stones** and pleasant things" (Daniel 11:38, emphasis added).

This can't be a coincidence. We also know that the place where the Antichrist demands worship of both himself and the image of the beast is in the temple in Jerusalem. Therefore, we can easily conclude that the items needed to be brought by the people of the world to worship the image of the beast in Jerusalem are gold, silver and precious stones.

So, consider that the Antichrist has demanded worship, and the way he says to worship is by offering gold, silver, and precious stones. Can you even imagine what that would do to the cost of these items in the global economy? If you thought the money changers and the people selling birds for sacrifice in the temple were bad, wait until they sell gold, silver, and precious stones to the pilgrims. Like I said, this will make the merchants richer than anyone ever has been.

Another group of goods mentioned as being sold to Mystery Babylon in Revelation 18 includes cinnamon, incense, fragrant oil, and frankincense. Each of these words is extremely rare in the Bible, and the words are only grouped together in one other context: they are the exact items God said to use to make the holy anointing oil to consecrate the temple and all the items in it. It was to be used to anoint the priests, too, and served an important role in temple services. The compound made from these items was considered so holy that God warned that no one should make any of it for any reason except for temple services; those who did so would be "cut off."

The next list of items in Revelation 18 is even more amazing: wine and oil, fine flour and wheat, cattle and sheep. These are the specific items needed to start the so-called daily sacrifice, a twice-daily sacrifice described in Exodus 29. Daniel 11 and 12 state that this particular sacrifice will again be started in the end times.

So you can see that when we take this section seriously, all of these items are clues that point to one thing: the temple and its services in Jerusalem. In my book, I go through all twenty-nine items that are sold to Mystery Babylon in the last days, and it's amazing to see how each of them points to this conclusion.

What Mystery Babylon Is Wearing

Even the items that the woman/city is wearing are far from random: "Alas, alas, that great city that was clothed in **fine linen, purple, and scarlet"** (Revelation 18:16a, emphasis added). These are all the specific colors that were to be worn by the high priest. This exact phrase is used dozens of times in Scripture. Even the idea that Mystery Babylon has a name written on her forehead is taken from the very same place where we find the description of the high priest's attire in Exodus 28. The high priest had a name written on his forehead, too, but it read "Holiness to the Lord."

Mystery Babylon, on the other hand, has the name "Mother of Harlots" written on her forehead.

The idea is that the city of Jerusalem is being pictured as a harlot-high priest, promoting the Antichrist as if he were their true God, causing the whole world to worship the Antichrist, in the way that a high priest should be promoting the worship of the true God.

Common Objections

Objection 1—What about the Seven Hills?

Many people say that Mystery Babylon sits on "seven hills," derived from their interpretation of Revelation 17:9–10:

> Here is the mind which has wisdom: The seven heads are seven mountains on which the woman sits. There are also seven kings. Five have fallen, one is, and the other has not yet come. And when he comes, he must continue a short time. (Revelation 17:9–10)

Many people say that this city on seven "hills" is Rome, which is famous for its seven hills. But that doesn't stop those who think Mystery Babylon is Mecca or even Jerusalem from claiming that their city also sits on seven hills. That all may be true, but the problem is that is not what this verse is talking about.

There are many ways to show the interpretation of this passage that I am about to suggest is true: grammatically, contextually, logically, and by comparing Scripture with Scripture. Let's start with grammar.

Revelation 17:9-10

(KJV) And here *is* the mind which hath wisdom. The seven heads are seven mountains, on which the woman sitteth. **And there are seven kings:** five are fallen, and one is, *and* the other is not yet come; and when he cometh, he must continue a short space.

(ESV) This calls for a mind with wisdom: the seven heads are seven mountains on which the woman is seated; **they are also seven kings**, five of whom have fallen, one is, the other has not yet come, and when he does come he must remain only a little while.

The key is the phrase "and there are seven kings." The excerpt indicates how the passage reads in the KJV. Other versions render this with a very important distinction. They say that the seven heads of the beast are seven mountains; however, the angel then further defines these mountains as being "seven kings": "They [the mountains] are **also** seven kings, five of whom have fallen, one is, the other has not yet come" (ESV, emphasis added).

We can see the difference. The KJV gives the idea that the angel begins to talk about a totally separate thing when he talks about the seven kings, whereas the ESV defines the seven mountains as *being* seven kings.

The difference in translations here is not an issue with the Greek texts, like the Textus Receptus or the Critical Text. The Greek manuscripts say the same thing here, so it's not one of *those* issues. This is simply a matter of translator choice.

There is near universal agreement among Bible translators that the seven mountains are in fact seven kings. In the following image, we see this is the way it is translated in almost every major English Bible.

Revelation 17:9-10

(ASV) and they are seven kings
(ESV) they are also seven kings,
(NIV) They are also seven kings.
(NASB) and they are seven kings
(HSB) They are also seven kings:
(RSV) they are also seven kings
(Geneva) They are also seuen King
(ERV) and they are seven kings
(NAB) and they are seven kings

Grammatically, a major reason for this is that the Greek word εἰ σ ιν *(eisin)* which in the KJV is translated as "there are" is the third-person plural of ε ιμι *(eimi),* meaning "I am," which should be rendered "they are." When describing the ten horns a few verses later, a similar phrase occurs: *deka basileis eisin*. There, the KJV and NKJV translate the phrase correctly, without substituting "there" for "they," as is done in verse 10.

Revelation 17:9-10

And here *is* the mind which hath wisdom. The seven heads are **seven mountains**, on which the woman sitteth. And **there are** εἰσιν [eisin] **seven kings:** five are fallen, and one is, *and* the other is not yet come; and when he cometh, he must continue a short space. - Rev 17:9-10 (KJV)

And **the ten horns** which thou sawest **are ten kings**, - Rev 17:12a

I am not a Greek scholar, and I wouldn't want anyone to believe me based solely on my grammatical explanation, so let's move on to showing that the angel is indicating that the seven mountains are seven kings by the context of the passage and by comparing Scripture with other Scripture.

I want to reiterate that all the other times in chapter 17 that the seven-headed beast with ten horns is mentioned, John seems to go out of his way to use phrases that were used back in Revelation 13. We know the beast in Revelation 13 has many of the same characteristics as the one in Revelation 17. They both have seven heads and ten horns, they both have names of blasphemy on their heads, they both are referred to by their having been killed yet living, they both have the earth dwellers "wonder" at them when they see their apparent resurrection, and they both have people whose names were not written in the Book of Life worship them. I know this seems obvious, but the view that the seven mountains are seven hills of a city prevents people from seeing the most basic point—that the seven-headed, ten-horned beast in Revelation 17 is the same beast of Revelation 13, which is obviously the Antichrist.

Our passage goes on to say that one of these heads, which are kings, is the same king who "was and is not" (Revelation 13) who gets the mortal wound. Let's flip back to Revelation 13:3 to check it out: "One of its heads seemed to have a mortal wound, but its mortal wound was healed, and the whole earth marveled as they followed the beast."

We see here that one of the beast's seven heads is said to have a mortal wound. This is an exact match with the Revelation 17 beast. Therefore, Revelation 17:9 has nothing to do with physical hills in Rome, Mecca, Jerusalem, or anywhere else. I mean, do you really think that one of the hills in Rome is going to be mortally wounded and then come back to life, or that everyone marvels at and begins to worship a hill? In other words, the woman/city is riding the Antichrist. This passage is not conveying the type of ground she is sitting on; she *is* the city, and she is riding the Antichrist, not hills.

Objection 2—Found No More

One of the best arguments against the theory that Jerusalem is Mystery Babylon is rooted in the following verse:

> And a mighty angel took up a stone like a great millstone, and cast it into the sea, saying, 'Thus with violence shall that great city Babylon be thrown down, and **shall be found no more at all.**" (Revelation 18:21, emphasis added)

The argument here is that Jerusalem can't be Mystery Babylon, because this passage says that it shall be found "no more at all," and we know that Jerusalem is in existence during the millennial reign. We also see the so-called New Jerusalem in the eternal kingdom. This is a very good argument, and it requires a very good answer. How can I say on the one hand that Jerusalem will be destroyed and be "found no more," and on the other hand say that it will be around forever?

The answer lies in the last eight chapters of the book of Ezekiel, where we find one of the most intricate, detailed building plans for the Israel of the Millennium. Ezekiel contains chapters and chapters of technical details regarding how Israel will be divided, the new temple complex, and Jerusalem and its surrounding areas. To say this is different than what we currently see in Israel is a bit of an understatement.

There are those who have taken all the technical specifications of things like the division of the land in the millennial reign and plotted it all on a map. The twelve tribes of Israel are given parallel rectangular allotments of land, one on top of the other, from the north border of Israel to the south, and each tribe's allotment extends along the entire east/west border of Israel. It really helps to see this all on a map to visualize what I'm saying.

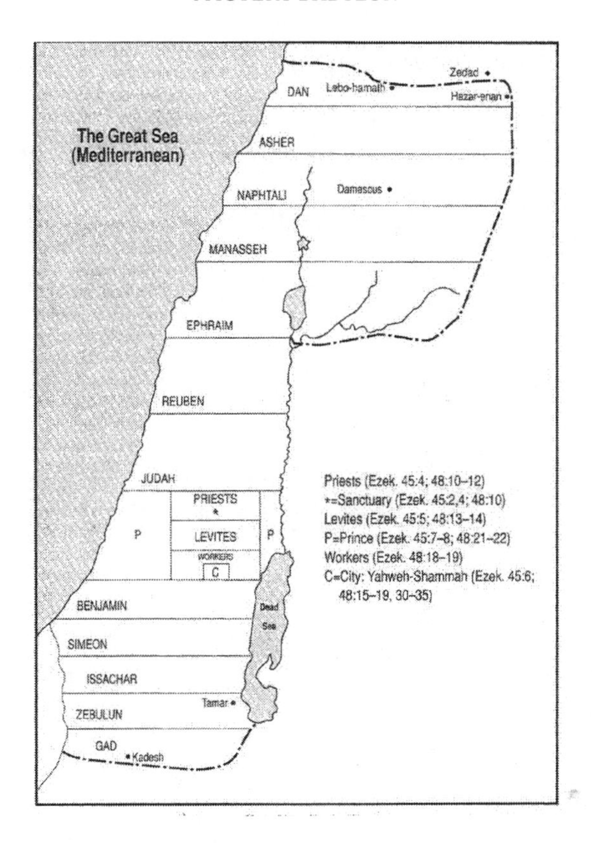

In the middle of these allotments of land is a rectangular portion that Ezekiel calls the "holy portion." The priests and Levites who service the temple equally divide this land. There is some debate as to where exactly the temple is in this section. Some say it is in the middle of this land and others say that it is just north of the city, but it doesn't appear to actually be in the city itself, which is very different from Jerusalem now.

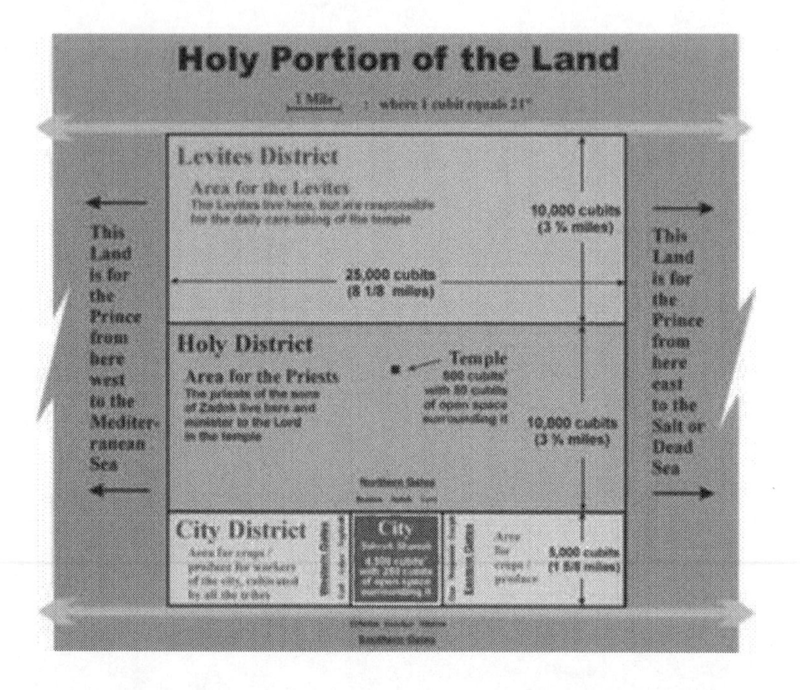

In addition, the city of Jerusalem is most likely also very different in physical location during the Millennium. It is perfectly square, and it is about nine times larger than Jerusalem is today. It has twelve gates—three on each side—and sits on a high plateau. Two rivers flow from it: the one on its east side flows to the Dead Sea and the one to its west flows all the way to the Mediterranean Sea. This Jerusalem is a different place; in fact, the last words in the book of Ezekiel give this Jerusalem a different name: "It was round about eighteen thousand measures: and the name of the city from that day shall be, The LORD is there" (Ezekiel 48:35). This is sometimes transliterated "YHWH Shammah," which means, "The Lord is there."

The city of Jerusalem's actual location in the Millennium is a matter of some debate. The people I am about to cite have no theological reason for saying that the location of the Jerusalem in the Millennial period (YHWH Shammah) is in a different location than the present city of Jerusalem. They do not, as far as I know, consider Mystery Babylon to be the last-days city of Jerusalem; they are simply trying to map out some of the details that Ezekiel gives in these eight chapters.

The International Standard Bible Encyclopedia gives two options based on the text, both of them south of Jerusalem. One of the possible locations is at Bethlehem and the other is a little farther north, but still south of Jerusalem, at modern-day Ramat Rahel.[32] Another researcher puts forward a good case for the millennial Jerusalem as being located at Shiloh, and another makes a case for Shechem.[33]

Even if the new city of Yahweh Shammah sat right on top of the old Jerusalem, we must at least conclude that it is nine times larger than the current city; therefore, it obviously does not contain the same physical landmarks and boundaries as the previous Jerusalem. And we know from various places in the Bible that it will sit on a large, raised platform—a long plateau that makes it visible from a very long way off. I have already mentioned that two rivers flow from it on either side, so we know that it's topographically not the same place, either. We start to get the idea that God will willingly call this city "Jerusalem," regardless of its not having the same features or physical location. Take, for example, the New Jerusalem of the eternal kingdom: It is called Jerusalem as well, despite it being a whopping fifteen hundred miles long.

---

32 Geoffrey W Bromiley, International Standard Bible Encyclopedia: E–J, (Eerdmans) 261.

33 C. MacKay, "Zechariah in Relation to Ezekiel 40–48," *Evangelical Quarterly* 40, 1968.

The judgment of the old city of Jerusalem described in the following passages may even create the topographical changes such as the plateau and the river that will run through the land.

> And there were voices, and thunders, and lightnings; and there was a great earthquake, such as was not since men were upon the earth, so mighty an earthquake, and so great. And the great city was divided into three parts, and the cities of the nations fell: and great Babylon came in remembrance before God, to give unto her the cup of the wine of the fierceness of his wrath. (Revelation 16:18–19)

As I noted in my previous book, this verse actually contrasts the "great city" (Mystery Babylon) with the "cities of the nations." This is a way to designate "the great city" as a non-Gentile city.

I also make the case that the reason the Lord splits the Mount of Olives, despite much confusion on this issue, is to make an escape route out of the old city of Jerusalem for the faithful remnant of Jews who are alive after the Day of the Lord. Consider in context this passage from the book of Zechariah:

> And his feet shall stand in that day upon the Mount of Olives, **which is before Jerusalem on the east**, and the Mount of Olives shall cleave in the midst thereof toward the east and toward the west, and there shall be a very great valley; and half of the mountain shall remove toward the north, and half of it toward the south. **And ye shall flee to the valley of the mountains; for the valley of the mountains shall reach unto Azal**: yea, ye shall flee, like as ye fled from before the earthquake in the days of Uzziah king of Judah: and the LORD my God shall come, and all the saints with thee. (Zechariah 14:4–5, emphasis added)

Why is the Lord getting the faithful to flee from Jerusalem with such extravagant measures in this moment of triumph? Is it because of the earthquake that is about to split the city in three parts, as described in Revelation 16?

> And there were noises and thunderings and lightnings; and there was a great earthquake, such a mighty and great earthquake as had not occurred since men were on the earth. Now the great city was divided into three parts, and the cities of the nations fell. And great Babylon was remembered before God, to give her the cup of the wine of the fierceness of His wrath. (Revelation 16:18–19)

Essentially, the old city of Jerusalem will be judged for promoting the worship of the Antichrist, among other things. It will be "found no more." But a much more glorious city of Jerusalem with a different size, location, and topography will continue at least until the point of the eternal kingdom, when once again a different kind of Jerusalem will overshadow the former.

Conclusions

If Mystery Babylon is Jerusalem, then it becomes one of the best places in Scripture to see what the kingdom of the Antichrist will look like in the end times. This validates many things I have been saying in this book—for example, that in the end times the Antichrist will try to make it look as if he is fulfilling the prophecies of the Messiah by making Jerusalem the capital city of the world and instituting the daily sacrifices again, as well as demanding people from all nations to go to Jerusalem to worship at the temple. The chapters that talk about Mystery Babylon describe just such a scene.

This concept also helps us understand something that is very difficult to comprehend: How is the Gentile world going to follow a Jewish Messiah? Isn't most of the world antagonistic toward Israel? This chapter shows us that the world is made "drunk" by the passion of Israel for their newfound Messiah. The world is drawn in, perhaps by the miracles of the False Prophet, or perhaps by the seeming fulfillment of so many Scriptures. Whatever the reason, the fact that the people are enticed into his worship by Jerusalem's own fornication with the Antichrist seems clear. This is not to say that the Antichrist will win over everyone. We have already seen he makes war against many nations who will not submit. He also institutes a plan known as the "mark of the Beast," which forces people to either worship him or die. So, not everyone will be "made drunk," but a great many people will be.

Chapter 5

Jewish Eschatology

I have already discussed many details about Jewish eschatology in this book, and I will presume that the reader already has a basic knowledge of the things I am about to discuss. This chapter will offer an overview of the basic beliefs of Jewish people regarding the end times and a comparison of these beliefs with the Bible. I will attempt to clearly lay out in chronological order how these particular beliefs could lead many Jews to respond to the Antichrist in a favorable way. I will then go in to some specific details about Jewish eschatology that I haven't yet had the opportunity to explain.

The basics of Jewish eschatology are essentially the same as the beliefs of most premillennial Christians. This is because Jewish people base most of what they believe about the end times on a text that is mutually shared with Christians: the Old Testament. The Old Testament contains a great deal of information about the last days. For example, Jews and premillennial Christians agree that there will be a time when the Messiah destroys the enemies of God, rules the world from Jerusalem, builds a third temple, and oversees a pilgrimage system enabling the Gentiles to go to Jerusalem to pay homage to that Messiah. The areas where Christians differ from Jews regard their beliefs about *how* the Messiah will do these things. The Jews get their information about how the Messiah will make these events happen primarily from sources other than the Bible, including various traditional texts like the Talmud and the writings of certain rabbis. In this chronology of events, I will limit myself to the beliefs that are the most widely held by the largest number of Jewish theologians, as well as just those events that directly pertain to the coming of the Messiah and His actions.

Messiah Ben Joseph's Wars

We have already discussed the fact that the Jews believe that two Messiahs will come in the last days (see chapter 3, "Wars of the Antichrist"). The first Messiah figure, Messiah ben Joseph, is said to fight great wars with the enemies of Israel and be completely victorious over them. In one sense, we could say that the first thing the Jewish world expects to see in the end times is a man to fight—and win—wars against Israel's enemies.

Biblical Connection:

I detailed in chapter 3 how Daniel 11:40–45 describes the Antichrist doing this exact thing as one of his first acts. He completely subdues all of Israel's major enemies, including Egypt and a coalition of Arab countries including Iran, Iraq, Syria, Turkey, and others.

Ben Joseph Killed In Jerusalem

After the major wars in which Israel's enemies are defeated, Messiah ben Joseph will be killed in the streets of Jerusalem. The length of time Messiah ben Joseph remains dead in the streets of Jerusalem differs; some say it will be as long as forty days.

The Jews see Zechariah 12:10 as speaking of this killing of Messiah ben Joseph just after his wars:[34]

> And I will pour on the house of David and on the inhabitants of Jerusalem the Spirit of grace and supplication; then they will look on Me whom they pierced. Yes, they will mourn for Him as one mourns for his only son, and grieve for Him as one grieves for a firstborn. (Zechariah 12:10)

The Jews see the word "they" as in "whom *they* pierced" as referring to the enemies of Israel who kill ben Joseph, as opposed seeing "they" as referring to "*they* themselves" who pierced Him, a reference to the killing of Jesus.

Biblical Connection:

Again, in chapter 3, I detailed how this is a direct chronological parallel with the Antichrist, who also, upon defeating the enemies of Israel, will go to Jerusalem, where he will be killed.

Resurrected

After Messiah ben Joseph is killed, he is said to be resurrected. Some say it will be Elijah who will resurrect Messiah ben Joseph, while others say it will be the new Messiah, Messiah ben David, who comes on the scene right at this point, who resurrects ben Joseph.

Biblical Connection:

---

[34] Talmud, Suk. 52a, b.

The resurrection of the Antichrist appears to be one of the main reasons the world follows him. I have argued in chapter 3 that this resurrection can be shown to occur in Jerusalem, directly after his wars against Israel's enemies and just before the abomination of desolation. In other words, here again we see a direct parallel to what the Bible says the Antichrist will do and what Jewish eschatology says Messiah ben Joseph will do.

Messiah Ben David Takes His Throne

After Messiah ben Joseph's resurrection, he seems to fade away from the scene. Messiah ben David, who is considered to be the superior Messiah, takes the throne in Jerusalem.

Biblical Connection:

After the resurrection of the Antichrist, he also takes his throne in the temple. I discussed this at length in the section of this book dealing with the abomination of desolation.

Ben David's Wars

According to Jewish eschatology, after Messiah ben David takes his throne, it will not immediately begin the time of peace that is believed to be on the horizon; in fact, this taking of the throne will begin a series of violent events. The first is said to be a war with the forces who killed ben Joseph. These forces are either Armilus' or Gog of Magog's, depending on whom you read. However, the fact that ben David will fight wars after he takes power is almost universal.

Biblical Connection:

While it is true that the Antichrist will gather all nations to fight the war of Armageddon three and a half years after the abomination of desolation, there is no clear indication from Scripture that I can see that he will immediately continue to subdue other countries after the abomination event. It would seem logical, however, that he would take steps to avenge those who killed him after he resurrects, thus fulfilling the Jewish expectations of this post-throne war. It is more likely that the killing of nonbelievers, which we will discuss in the next point, may serve to fulfill the Jewish expectations of this post-resurrection war—that is, a war against all those who will not accept him as their king. In fact, the Bible indeed calls the persecution of believers after this point a "war," saying that God permits the Antichrist to "make war on the saints" for three and a half years.

Killing of Nonbelievers

In Jewish eschatology, after Israel becomes supreme, it is seen as its duty to root out and kill all unrepentant Gentiles, those who will not submit to the Messiah as king. In other words, there is believed to be a time of religious genocide after Messiah ben David takes his throne.

Biblical Connection:

Jesus said that after the Antichrist takes his throne in the temple, a persecution will begin that will be unrivaled in all history.

Chronology Summary

The rabbinic teachings in Judaism about the Messiah's rise to power are so exactly paralleled to the Bible's description of the

Antichrist's rise to power that it's without question that the Jewish people will be extremely vulnerable to the deception of the Antichrist when these events come to pass.

Miscellaneous Points Regarding Jewish Eschatology

A few additional issues are germane to this chronology.

Ben David, Ben Joseph—The Same?

Should we expect two different Jewish Messiah figures as a part of this deception of the Antichrist? I believe the answer is no. I say that with some confidence, because the Bible makes no distinction between the Antichrist who fights the wars, dies, and resurrects and the one who takes the throne in the temple.

The entire idea of the two Messiahs only exists in the rabbinic tradition because the Jews wished to explain how the Messiah can die and be mourned, as is seen Zechariah 12:10. Obviously, they don't see this as referring to Jesus, so another explanation was required. They solved this by creating the idea of two Messiahs in the end times. I believe that when the Jews see the Antichrist resurrected, they will have no theological problem with accepting that there really is only one Messiah who fulfills all these prophecies and that they were wrong about the two-Messiahs idea. The theology may even be explained to them at that time in detail by the False Prophet, whom they will see as Elijah; or, it may be explained to them by the Antichrist himself. The idea of only one Messiah is much more theologically correct, anyway, and I suspect it will be no trouble at all for the Jews to agree to this more-correct doctrine as long as the Antichrist claims that he is descended from David, a point that I think is necessary in order for this deception to work on them. There may even be a scenario in which

Antichrist shows lineage from both Joseph and David, though I don't think this would be necessary.

A Dangerous Difference between Jewish Eschatology and the Bible

Rabbinic traditions of eschatology differ from the Bible on many points, but I would like to focus on one I believe Satan will exploit to great advantage. The Bible speaks of the Messiah's defeat of the enemies of Israel just before the Messianic Age. Christians and Jews agree on that basic point. The crucial difference is the *way* the Messiah will do this.

In the Bible, the Messiah will defeat these enemies alone, without the help of any humans; on the other hand, rabbinic tradition says this defeat of Israel's enemies will be carried out by a human king fighting conventional wars against certain countries that have oppressed Israel.

In chapter 19 of the book of Revelation, we see a picture of the supernatural war the real Messiah will fight. As we read it, notice that the armies that accompany Him are angelic, not human; and the war—if you can call it that, because it seems very one-sided—will be completely unlike anything that an earthly king or conventional army could do. Also notice the term "He Himself" that is used several times, as this will be important when we look at the Old Testament counterparts to this passage.

> **And the armies in heaven**, clothed in fine linen, white and clean, followed Him on white horses. Now out of **His mouth** goes a sharp sword, that with it **He should strike the nations**. And **He Himself** will rule them with a rod of iron. **He Himself** treads the winepress of the fierceness and wrath of Almighty God.... And the rest were killed with

> the sword **which proceeded from the mouth of Him who sat on the horse.** And all the birds were filled with their flesh. (Revelation 19:14–15, 19–21, emphasis added)

The idea that the destruction of the wicked before the Messianic Age would be accomplished by the Messiah himself is not just a New Testament idea. If the Jews restricted their view of this event to the Old Testament alone instead of rabbinic traditions, they could have also come to this conclusion.[35] For instance, several passages mirror the one we just read in Revelation 19, such as Isaiah 11:4–6 and Zechariah 14:3. In fact, I think that Isaiah 63 makes this point very clear.

Isaiah 62 talks about how God will deliver Israel from their enemies in the last days by the hand of the Messiah. Then, chapter 63 begins by speaking of how this event will happen. I will highlight the portions of this passage that make the point that "He alone," without earthly armies, accomplishes this mission:

> Who is this who comes from Edom, With dyed garments from Bozrah, This One who is glorious in His apparel, Traveling in the greatness of His strength?—"I who speak in righteousness, mighty to save."
>
> Why is Your apparel red, And Your garments like one who treads in the winepress? "**I have trodden the winepress alone**, And **from the peoples no one was with Me**. For I

[35] Certain passages like Micah 5:5–6 and others suggest that human fighting can happen during the Millennium, usually as a part of Israel's ruling over the surrounding nations. However, the point being made in this section is that when the Bible speaks of the particular war/fighting that is to occur just before the Millennium, when God/the Messiah/Jesus judges the enemies of Israel, it is not spoken of as needing human help.

> **have trodden** them in My anger, And trampled them in My fury; Their blood is sprinkled upon My garments, And **I have stained all My robes**. For the day of vengeance is in My heart, And the year of My redeemed has come. **I looked, but there was no one to help**, And I wondered That there was no one to uphold; Therefore **My own arm brought salvation** for Me; And **My own fury**, it sustained Me. **I have trodden down the peoples** in My anger, Made them drunk **in My fury, And brought down their strength to the earth."** (Isaiah 63:1–6, emphasis added)

It could be argued that the main point of this passage is to say that He alone will pour out vengeance upon the nations. It's essentially a direct rebuke of the idea that earthly armies will be needed to destroy Israel's enemies.

This declaration of his independent conquering of the nations is not mutually exclusive to the idea that angelic armies will be present, as mentioned in Revelation 19. This is because of the phrase in Isaiah 63 that says "from the peoples no one was with Me," which may simply mean that there were no human armies with him. The passages that clarify that the angelic armies are a part of the judgment of the nations just before the Messianic Age are numerous. One example is from Matthew 25:31: "When the Son of Man comes in His glory, and **all the holy angels** with Him, **then He will sit on the throne of His glory"** (emphasis added; also see Matthew 16:27, 13:39; Zechariah 14:5; Mark 8:38; Luke 9:26; and 2 Thessalonians 1:7–10).

This conquering of Israel's enemies with angelic armies is obviously something no human can fulfill. The belief of the Jews that their Messiah will come on the scene by fighting human wars with human armies is dangerous, because it plays right into the hands of Satan, who can easily orchestrate human wars. As a result of this tradition about Messiah ben Joseph, all Satan has to do is provoke a Muslim attack and help the Antichrist defeat those armies. It will be almost too easy for him to have the Antichrist declared the Messiah because of these low expectations.

We now need to take a look at the eschatological beliefs of Islam, and see that they, too, will play a role in the end-times deception of the Antichrist.

Chapter 6

Islamic Eschatology

I believe that Islamic eschatology will also play an important role during the last days, but not in the way many Christians today think it will. Most of the ideas we are going to discuss about Islamic end-times beliefs come not from the Quran, the central text in Islam, but from the hadiths, a word that means "tradition." The hadiths are a collection of sayings attributed to Mohammed, compiled by his companions over the course of the hundreds of years after his death in AD 632. Even within Islam, many of these hadiths are considered spurious. By the ninth century, the number of these sayings had grown exponentially, some of them clearly contradicting each other. Islamic scholars had to decide which ones were authentic and which had been invented for political or theological purposes.[36]

I will briefly outline a few key points regarding Islamic eschatology and make some general comments on them. As in the section on Jewish eschatology, I will limit my overview of the subject to the most common and widely held beliefs about the end times in Islam.

---

[36] John L. Esposito. "Islam: The Straight Path." 81. 4th ed. Oxford University Press, 2010.

The Mahdi

The Mahdi is the central figure in Islamic eschatology. In the simplest terms, he will restore spiritual greatness to Islam and fight various wars with its enemies. He will unite Islam spiritually and militarily and have power for seven, nine, or nineteen years (according to different views).[37] He is expected to come on the scene first.

Al-Masih ad-Dajjal

The Dajjal is the bad guy in Islamic eschatology. He is a man who claims to be the Jewish Messiah and will gain many converts to this idea. In fact, that's what "Al-Masih ad-Dajjal" means: "imposter Messiah." Various hadiths have described him as a grotesque figure, often making mention of him as blind in one eye, though some say this is symbolic language used to refer to his singular focus on ruling the world. He will gain considerable control over the world, and will only be able to be stopped by the next character on our list, Isa.

Isa

This is the Muslim version of Jesus, who is believed to be a prophet but not God. Muslims believe, as do Christians, that he is coming back again, but they see him as coming back to be a subordinate to the Mahdi. The main thing Isa will do in Islamic eschatology is kill the Dajjal. It is said that he will return on a mountaintop outside Israel as the Mahdi's armies are preparing to go to war against the Dajjal. Isa is said to kill the Dajjal during this

---

[37] Richard C. Martin, ed. (2004), "Mahdi," *Encyclopedia of Islam and the Muslim World,* Thompson Gale, p. 421.

battle. Also, Isa is supposed to be a great help in converting many Christians to Islam. He is said to rule the world after the war until he dies at a good old age.

Holy Wars

Many wars are fought in Islamic eschatology, such as the defeat of Constantinople and many other cities by the Mahdi. However, no war is more important than the war that must be fought against the Jews and their false messiah (the Dajjal), because the Muslims believe the last hour will not come until they do. A very famous hadith says:

> Abu Huraira reported Allah's Messenger (may peace be upon him) as saying: The last hour would not come unless the Muslims will fight against the Jews and the Muslims would kill them until the Jews would hide themselves behind a stone or a tree and a stone or a tree would say: Muslim, or the servant of Allah, there is a Jew behind me; come and kill him; but the tree Gharqad would not say, for it is the tree of the Jews.[38]

I believe this need to fight an end-times war against the Jews and the Dajjal will play a very important part of the Antichrist's end-times deception, which I will explain in greater detail later in this book.

---

[38] Sahih Muslim 41:6985; see also Sahih Muslim 41:6981, Sahih Muslim 41:6982, Sahih Muslim 41:6983, Sahih Muslim 41:6984, and Sahih Bukhari 4:56:791.

Modern Christian Views of Islamic Eschatology

A view that has become very popular among Christians is that Islamic eschatology will come to pass more or less as Muslims claim it will, except the man the Muslims will call the Mahdi is really the Antichrist, the man they will say is Isa is really the False Prophet, and the man they claim to be the Dajjal is the real Jesus. I understand why they think this; in fact, I used to believe it, too, but I now think the view is wrong and even quite dangerous.

The reason I say it's dangerous should be obvious to the reader at this point. If even half of what I am saying in this book is true, then I can't think of a more dangerous teaching than one stating that Christians should embrace a man who fights human wars against the Muslims, defeats them, and declares himself to be the Jewish Messiah. In other words, if I am right, then this Islamic Antichrist view is essentially preparing Christians to embrace the Antichrist.

The reason the view is attractive to Christians is because it's simple to understand. After all, the Muslims have a guy (the Mahdi) who looks just like the Antichrist in that he is supposed to rule the world and kill Jews and Christians. Not just that, he also has a subordinate sidekick who is claiming to be Jesus, which, with some tweaking, can look just like the biblical False Prophet. (For more on why I think these Christians are wrong about saying the False Prophet will claim to be Jesus, see the section in the appendix titled "Two Horns Like a Lamb.") There is even talk of things like a seven-year peace agreement. It sounds like an open-and-shut case, but there are a number of logical reasons such similarities aren't really as amazing as people think.

As I mentioned before, most, if not all, of these beliefs come from the hadiths, which are supposedly sayings of Mohammed recorded by his followers hundreds of years after his death; some of them were written closer to AD 1000. Most, if not all, of the men who wrote Islamic eschatology, therefore, were aware of Christian end-times beliefs. I suggest that for the most part, all they were doing was taking Christian eschatology, reversing the roles, and calling it Islamic doctrine. For example, as I mentioned, one hadith talks about a seven-year peace agreement in the end times. It reads as follows:

> There will be four peace agreements between you and the Romans. The fourth agreement will be mediated through a person who will be from the progeny of Hadhrat [Aaron, Moses' brother, i.e., a Jew] and will be upheld for seven years.[39]

This is seen as a peace agreement between Christians and Muslims, mediated by a Jew from the priest class. One hadith even says the Christians/Jews will break this covenant and attack Muslims despite the agreement, which is obviously a parallel to the Antichrist breaking the seven-year covenant.

This hadith is quoted by many Christian authors as proof that the Antichrist will be a Muslim. Such theories are overlooking the obvious fact that these writers were doing little more than reading what the Bible says about the end times, making the same claims with a few additions, and, most importantly, casting Muslims as the good guys and Jews and Christians as the bad guys.

The person who wrote this particular peace-agreement hadith was al-Tabarani, who died in AD 970, almost nine hundred years after the book of Revelation was written. He was a major student of Christianity; in fact, Christian doctrine was kind of his specialty.

---

[39] Tabrani, Ref: Kanz-ul-Aamal, Page 268, Hadith No. 3868.

To put it another way, he knew all about the Christian belief in a seven-year covenant that would be broken by the Antichrist in the end times. All al-Tabarani did was switch the roles and say that the people who will break the covenant, which in the Bible is the Antichrist, will be the Jews and Christians. He just switched the roles.

Any student of Islam knows that taking Bible stories and switching the roles to benefit Islam is a major aspect of Islamic doctrine. For example, Islam retells the story of Abraham taking Isaac to Mt. Moriah for a sacrifice by saying that it is Ishmael (the father of the Muslim nations) rather than Isaac whom Abraham takes. The official position of Islam is that the Bible, while still containing the basic truth, has been corrupted by the Jews and Christians. Muslims feel this gives them a license to make these role reversals consistently in order to make themselves out to be the good guys and the Christians and Jews the bad guys.

So you can see why the end-times scenarios of Islam are so similar to Christian beliefs. Christians believe that in the end times, the good guy (Jesus) will kill unbelievers and set up a world government. Simply changing the roles has the good guy being a Muslim, killing unbelievers (who, in this case, are Christians and Jews), and setting up a world government. That sounds like the Antichrist, right? That's what happens when you reverse the roles; it's not rocket science.

This modern Islamic Antichrist view held by many Christians today, which I will address in more detail in later chapters, is primarily based on the belief that the Muslims know better about how the end times will play out than the Bible does. I know that sounds harsh, but it's true. For instance, Christians who hold to this view are accepting as a fact that there really will be a fake Jesus who will come back and be the sidekick to a Muslim king, as the hadiths say. They then have to force this notion on biblical concepts. For example, in their view, the False Prophet will pretend to be Jesus. The Bible certainly never says this, nor do I believe that the False Prophet's actions imply it. But they have forced this doctrine on the Bible. This is what I mean when I say that in a way they are giving more stock to what the hadiths say about the end times than to what the Bible says.

What Is Satan's Plan for Islamic Eschatology?

As I mentioned at the beginning of this chapter, I do think that Satan plans to use the end-times beliefs of Muslims to his advantage in the last days, but not in the way that most Christians think. I believe he plans to use the belief that Muslims must unite to fight a war against the Dajjal (the man who claims to be the Jewish Messiah). In other words, regardless of whether a Mahdi or Isa figure shows up, a kind of Dajjal (the Antichrist) certainly will. This obvious appearance of a Jewish Messiah figure, who they will no doubt interpret to be the Dajjal, will trigger the Muslim war the Antichrist needs, regardless of whether nothing else they believe will happen comes to pass.

Daniel 11:40–45 makes it clear that the Antichrist is attacked first by the Muslim world. His defeat of the attacking Muslim armies is the major catalyst that will propel him to his unquestioned acceptance as the Messiah—certainly by the Jews, and, I fear, by some Christian groups as well. All Satan needs from the Muslim world is to provoke it to attack him en masse. The Antichrist is said to be empowered by his "god of fortresses" specifically to fight wars, so he is not worried about the military threat from the Muslims at all, but he needs them to attack him so he can look like the savior of Israel. Islamic eschatology regarding the Dajjal, all by itself, is the eschatological time bomb that will give the Antichrist the war he needs to look like the Messiah.

I suppose it is possible that those in the Muslim world will choose from among themselves a Mahdi figure during this time to lead the war against the Antichrist, but I don't think it is biblically necessary. In fact, based on Daniel 11:41, the Islamic attacks come from at least two different kings—the kings of the north and the south. So, I doubt the kind of unification of the Muslim world under one military leader such as the Mahdi will happen. If a man does claim to be the Mahdi, though, he will be defeated by the Antichrist, whom they see as the Dajjal, almost as soon as he shows up, and the Muslim world will realize it has been deceived early on. I do think that the Antichrist would find a lot of use for a type of patsy Muslim Antichrist to defeat, especially if he plans on using such a notion to deceive Christians who need an Antichrist to be defeated before they will accept anyone as a candidate for Jesus. For that reason, I don't dismiss the idea of a patsy/Antichrist/Mahdi figure altogether, though it's not something the Bible talks about, from what I have seen.

The Islamic Antichrist idea that has become so popular is based on a number of other factors besides Islamic eschatology, and I will do my best to address most of those ideas in later chapters. In the next chapter, however, I will try to make some sense of all these eschatological beliefs among Jews, Christians, and Muslims, and will try to lay out a possible scenario that will show how they will all work together to further the Antichrist's goals.

Chapter 7

The Disastrous Results of Jewish and Islamic Eschatology

In attempting to come up with a chronological scenario that takes into account all we have learned so far, I will admittedly be speculating quite a bit. This is because, no doubt, many unanticipated geopolitical events will happen between now and then. Therefore I ask the reader to take this attempt at a chronology of events with a grain of salt, understanding that I expect some of the things I am about to say to ultimately be proven wrong. That said, I do think that we can get a pretty good idea of how this will all look when it comes to pass, even if some of the minor details can't be fully known.

The Seven-Year Covenant

While certain events can be inferred to happen before the covenant that the Antichrist makes in Daniel 9:27, biblically speaking, we have to start the end-times narrative from this traditional starting point. I argued earlier that I believe this covenant is an attempt to mimic the new covenant mentioned in Jeremiah 31:31 that the Jews are awaiting the Messiah to make with them. This covenant would begin a massive reinvigoration of the Jewish laws and rituals in Israel. I also argued that the text in Daniel suggests that the covenant will include the reinstatement of the daily sacrifice. If this view of the covenant made by the Antichrist is true, then we can infer that this event will be of monumental proportions and is much bigger and broader than a simple peace treaty.

For one thing, this means the Antichrist is claiming to be the Messiah at this point, or at least doing things to make people infer that he is. I say this because the concept of the new covenant in Jeremiah is something that must be done by the Messiah, both in Christian and Jewish belief. In addition, the construction of the temple is also believed possible only when the Messiah comes, though it is true that certain Jews today believe they don't have to wait on the Messiah to build the temple. The majority of religious Jews disagree on that point. We know that this covenant is made by the Antichrist, so it seems logical to assume that one of the first things we will see is this covenant with a Messiah figure and the reinvigoration of Jewish laws and rituals. The Jews claiming to have found their Messiah and starting work on the temple will be quite a spectacle; all eyes will be on Israel 24/7 from that moment on.

This brings up several difficult questions concerning the False Prophet, who will almost certainly claim to be the biblical Elijah. In Jewish thought, it is inconceivable that a person could be accepted as the Messiah without being introduced by Elijah. It would seem, therefore, that the False Prophet will appear at the time of this covenant or before. Since many Jews believe it will be Elijah who helps them with the difficult theological questions concerning the specifics of the rebuilding of the temple, this seems like perfect timing anyway.

It may be that the Antichrist appears on the world stage before the covenant and becomes well known through political or military exploits in another part of the world. Such a view seems logical, because we wouldn't expect the Antichrist to appear out of nowhere declaring himself to be the Messiah to the Jews. In fact, I submit that his early career, spoken of in Daniel 7 about his coming from a ten-king confederacy after subduing three of them, accounts for his being well known in one way or another before the covenant. The False Prophet then would also come on the scene during this pre-covenant time, gain support in Israel in some way for his claim to be Elijah, and become widely respected. Then, just before this amazing covenant is made, the False Prophet tells everyone that the man who has been making waves on the world stage recently is their Messiah. It's possible that all this would be happening during a time when Israel is feeling threatened by its enemies.

The Islamic Time Bomb

In these early stages, no group will be paying more attention to this monumental development in Israel than the Muslims. Even if, as some believe, a way to construct the temple next to the Dome of the Rock is possible (without tearing it down), there is no scenario in which the events that follow the covenant don't awaken the preprogrammed eschatological passions of the Islamic world.

The Temple Mount is currently controlled by the Muslims, even though Israel technically has sovereignty over the site. Today, you can't be caught bringing a Bible or praying anywhere on the Temple Mount, let alone building an altar and sacrificing animals to Yahweh. Starting the daily sacrifice on the Temple Mount is just not going to go over well at all with the Muslims. I suspect that if the Jews really believe their Messiah has come, then they also believe that he is about to go to war with and conquer their enemies. So, the one thing that has prevented them from building the temple in the past—imminent war with all Muslims—will cease to be a problem for them, as they believe the Messiah will protect them, and they might even welcome the chance to defeat the Muslims in the epic war that this action will cause. If the Antichrist has a proven military background, this may add to their confidence about this impending war.

It's not just the rebuilding of the temple that will guarantee a war with Islam. It is also the Islamic belief in a coming Dajjal (the false Jewish Messiah) that will inflame their passions to go to war with Israel en masse at this time. The Antichrist will be well aware of the consequences of these actions, and will actually be counting on such a war. As far as Satan sees it, the bigger the number of Muslim armies that attack the Antichrist, the better, because he is attempting to make it seem like the Antichrist is fulfilling the messianic prophecies of the destruction of Israel's enemies.

I mentioned that I'm not sure if these Islamic armies will be led by a single man or not; the Bible seems to suggest that they won't. That being said, if the Muslims believe the Dajjal is on the scene, it seems logical that they would choose someone to act as a Mahdi, even if he doesn't exactly fit all the criteria they were expecting. Remember that Isa isn't even expected to come on the scene until the Muslims are already involved in this war, so they certainly won't be waiting on him to show up. I personally think he never will, but I am open to being wrong on this point. As I said in the previous chapter, if such characters like a Mahdi and Isa do emerge during this time, the group that will be the most deceived by them will be the Christians who, believing they have found an Antichrist and False Prophet to hate, will by default be ready to accept the man who defeats them, which will be the real Antichrist.

The Victories of the False Messiah

According to Daniel 11:40–45, the battles between Antichrist and the Muslim nations occur outside of Israel. This is consistent with the Jewish belief that the wars of Messiah ben Joseph are fought in the desert, meaning that the Antichrist, after the covenant is made and temple construction begins, leaves Israel to go to war with the Muslim armies that will have been so angered by the recent events. Daniel says that although the Antichrist is attacked first, he will have no trouble at all defeating his enemies. What's interesting is that it seems from the Bible's description of these victories that there is something about the way he fights wars that is so utterly impossible to defend that the nations he defeats become totally submissive to him. They fall under his full control after they see his war-making powers. I suspect that because of Satan's help, the Antichrist is able to demonstrate something completely new with his warfare. Maybe it's supernatural, maybe it's technological, but I believe the verse that asks, "Who is like the beast, who can make war with him?" in Revelation 13:4 reflects a sentiment that will be felt by the whole world. This inability for him to be defeated in war will ultimately cause the entire world to come under his control.

After the Muslim armies are defeated, it will then be safe for Jews worldwide to return to Israel. This is something they probably would have wanted to do when the covenant was made, but it was obvious that a major war would result from those actions. Once they see that the coast is clear and all enemies are pacified, the Jews worldwide will begin to migrate to Israel en masse.

The Ingathering

One of the most important Jewish beliefs about Messiah ben Joseph is that after the wars he fights in the desert, he will lead many Jews back to the land of Israel. Nahmanides, one of the most influential Jewish sages in the Middle Ages, orders the events as follows: "[Messiah Ben Joseph will appear,] wipe out idolatry, **gather in Israel**, **lead them to the Holy Land**" (emphasis added).[40]

This is consistent with the Antichrist's movements after the initial defeat of the kings of the north and south, because just after those wars, he marches toward the Holy Land, too. As I argued in chapter 3, this march to Jerusalem is in victory, not aggression, evidenced by the fact that once he gets there, he seems to be taking on all of Israel's "micro enemies," those lands that directly occupy the areas around Israel, although most of Jordan will apparently "escape from his hands." It therefore can be postulated that Antichrist's defeat of the Palestinian coastlands and the rest of Israel's immediate but less serious enemies may be to make room for the masses of Jewish exiles who will be pouring in to Israel after he subdues the Muslim world. Right now, more Jews live in the USA than in Israel. If Antichrist plans on fulfilling the prophecies of the ingathering of the people, he is going to need a bigger Israel, and it explains this apparent real-estate grab after the major wars.

There appear to be more conquests to the east and north during this time, too. It is conceivable that the Antichrist is trying to extend the borders of Israel at this point to the borders mentioned in Genesis 15:18–21, "from the brook of Egypt to the Euphrates,"

---

[40] Saracheck, 175.

which would include all of modern-day Israel, the Palestinian territories, Lebanon, Syria, Jordan, and Iraq, as well as Kuwait, Saudi Arabia, United Arab Emirates, Oman, Yemen, most of Turkey, and all of the land east of the Nile River. Or, at least he is trying to expand to the less significant but still greater borders of the old Davidic dynasty. This is speculation, however, and the reason that the Antichrist goes to war in the east and north before his apparent assassination in Israel could simply be for defensive reasons. Regardless of his reasons, he will be as victorious as before and presumably able to do what he wants with the lands he conquers after this.

The Killing of the Antichrist

The killing of the Antichrist (the first time) and why it is done is a mystery in the Bible. He certainly will be making many enemies around the world at this point, so it could be any number of candidates. Regardless of who does it, he receives his "mortal head wound" in Israel just after the previously mentioned wars. His killing does not appear to be the result of an invading army (as is the case in Islamic belief), because the Bible doesn't mention any more attacks from outsiders at this point. I lean toward an individual assassin doing this, but, again, the Bible is not clear on the subject.

Just prior to the killing of the Antichrist, the Muslim world will certainly be confused and disheartened, because much of what they believed was going to happen in the end times will not be panning out. They are being defeated on all fronts by the man they surely will see as the Dajjal. I submit that they will be even more disappointed as the rest of the events unfold, but this killing of the Dajjal (the Antichrist) will be one last glimmer of hope that maybe their end-times texts were right. After all, the Dajjal was supposed to be killed, in their view, and now he has been. Granted, this killing is supposed to be done by the Muslim Jesus during a great battle, but I'm sure they can find a way to accommodate the less-than-literal fulfillment of this prophecy.

The Jewish people, on the other hand, though disheartened by the death of the man they believe is their redeemer, will no doubt be cautiously optimistic at this point. This, after all, will be exactly what they believed would happen. The death of the Messiah in Israel just after the wars and the ingathering is simply the next step in the process. They will believe that all they have to do is mourn him in accordance with Zechariah 12:10 and he will be resurrected. Unfortunately for everyone, they will not be disappointed.

A Resurrection That Changes Everything

We should take a moment to consider the theological problem the resurrection of the Antichrist poses. I do not believe that Satan has the power to raise the dead, but at the same time, I don't see any way around the many verses that say the Antichrist really dies; it just doesn't seem to allow for a fake death to me. I recommend the paper, "Can Satan Raise the Dead? Toward a Biblical View of the Beast' s Wound" by Gregory H. Harris to anyone who's interested in this subject. To sum the paper up, it seems that God is the one who resurrects the Antichrist for the purpose of condemning those who do not believe the truth. In 2 Thessalonians 2, we find the following verse, which I believe states that God is the one who sends the "strong delusion" that, in this view, is the resurrection of the Antichrist:

> The coming of the lawless one is according to the working of Satan, with all power, signs, and lying wonders, and

> with all unrighteous deception among those who perish, because they did not receive the love of the truth, that they might be saved. And for this reason **God will send them strong delusion, that they should believe the lie, that they all may be condemned who did not believe the truth** but had pleasure in unrighteousness. (2 Thessalonians 2:9–12, emphasis added)

The Bible is silent about whether another man acts as if he resurrects the Antichrist. As I mentioned, many Jews believe it will be Elijah or ben David who resurrects Messiah ben Joseph, but all we're told in the Bible is that it happens. This resurrection is a major turning point in the end-times chronology. Until this moment, Muslims may have held out some hope that their view of the end times was correct. But because of a resurrected "Dajjal" and the complete subjection of most, if not all, Muslim countries, they will hopefully begin to see that they have been deceived by their religion. I hold out great hope for a massive Muslim revival at this point. I fully expect that many of the Muslims still alive will turn to Christianity, though it will be at the cost of their lives, as we will soon see.

After the resurrection, Christians who may have been deceived in one way or another until this event will also start to wake up. Perhaps they will have been toying with the idea that this man was the return of Jesus. Or, if the Antichrist doesn't claim to be Jesus, perhaps they will have been starting to believe that this man was the real Messiah and Jesus wasn't. In any case, after the resurrection of the Antichrist, an event that is so antithetical to Christian doctrine, and something that Scripture clearly attributes to the Antichrist, I expect a mass awaking among Christians to occur as well.

Though this event will be a time when some people will realize the true nature of the Antichrist, it will also be a time for others to embrace the Antichrist with their whole being. Regardless of which side of that fence people will fall, it's about to be illegal for anyone to oppose the Antichrist, and refusal to worship him will soon be punishable by death.

The Temple Is Ready

After the resurrection of the Antichrist—perhaps directly after—he declares himself to be God in the temple. I don't know if this is something he would have done earlier if he could have; I don't know if the temple was fully constructed before this time. In any case, he does so at the midpoint of the seven-year period, and this is when his theology also seems to change.

We know that at this point he stops the daily sacrifices, which he himself seems to have established three and a half years earlier. In exchange, he sets up an image of himself, the so-called image of the beast. He also declares himself to be divine. I argued in an earlier chapter that this declaration of his divinity and the setting up of the image may be an attempt not for him to break from the pretense of Judaism, as is often suggested, but rather to bolster his messianic claims. Both actions are in effect closer to the doctrine of the biblical Messiah than his previous theology. The Messiah, as Christians are aware, is in fact God, so this new declaration of divinity may be backed up with Scripture. And as for the image of himself in the temple, I argued that even this step is an attempt to more accurately reflect the important messianic doctrine that the Messiah will rule from the temple during the Millennium and receive the offerings from the pilgrims who will flow to Jerusalem. Since the Antichrist cannot waste time by sitting in the temple himself, he sets up this image to try to fulfill this important prophecy. In effect, he is reinforcing his messianic claims with these actions, though the main difference is that he now requires worship.

In the place of the daily sacrifice, he will institute an obligatory offering of gold, silver, and precious stones to the image of the beast. The image has the power to kill those pilgrims who will not worship it. I personally believe that Satan will indwell this image for the purpose of receiving worship, but this is pure speculation.

Time to Make a Decision

The persecution that follows the abomination of desolation is described as the worst in history. We are told in effect that this persecution has its epicenter in Jerusalem, and that it begins immediately after the abomination of desolation—so immediately, in fact, that people must flee at all cost when they see the abomination, and with great speed if they want to avoid the persecution. These facts suggest that many people in Jerusalem will not see what the Antichrist does as an abomination at all. The speed in which they carry out the Antichrist's orders to kill believers suggests great zeal on their part. We can only infer the reasons the Antichrist will give for his order to have believers rounded up and killed, but, as I have noted previously, many Jews believe that when the Messiah comes, there will be a need for just such an extermination of unbelievers. This belief in the need for an eschatological genocide is different from the belief that the Messiah will make war on Israel's neighbors prior to him sitting on the throne of David. This particular killing is expected to happen after those wars and after the final Messiah, Messiah ben David, takes his throne. Many Jews believe that at that point they will need to root out and kill all those who are left who won't submit to the rule of the Messiah in order to usher in the final and everlasting peace.[41] There will be a very attractive motive for the people to carry out the persecution of unbelievers. The feeling of the day will be: "Kill all unbelievers or the Utopia cannot come."

At this point, the Antichrist really will rule the world. I believe this is when he institutes programs like the mark of the Beast, which will prevent those who don't have it from buying and selling, beginning the great choice for the rest of the world: Accept the mark and worship the Beast or die. Even though many people might not be convinced of Antichrist's divine claims at this point, many people, regardless of their religious beliefs, will take the mark out of convenience, to preserve their lives, or both. Only Christians and those Jews who will hear the pleas of the two witnesses will refuse the mark and either be killed or go into hiding.

Though much more happens after this, I will end this chronology here, as these are the events that most pertain to the rise of the Antichrist and the thesis of this book.

---

[41] Joseph Sarachek. *The Doctrine of the Messiah in Medieval Jewish Literature*, p. 19.

Chapter 8

Will the Antichrist Be a Roman?

Despite what many of us have been taught, Scripture does not teach us that the Antichrist will come from Rome. Nevertheless, I believe that he *could* come from Rome or a European Union-type of organization. Although this is possible, I hope to demonstrate that it is not taught in Scripture. In fact, I'm not sure whether Scripture tells us exactly which kingdom or kingdoms the Antichrist comes from other than that it will be a nation or nations with ten rulers, three of which he will "subdue" on his way to power (Daniel 7:8, 24). This nation (or nations) is outside of Israel, and is probably in the west, because Antichrist fights with the kings of the north and south as well as with people from the east (Daniel 11:40–45). Other than that, I don't think we are told exactly where Antichrist will originate.

Further, even if I believed that the Antichrist will be Roman, it would not detract from the thesis of this book at all. A Jewish leader could rise in the ranks of an organization such as the European Union or almost any other nation, especially if he is as skilled as the Antichrist will apparently be. So, to restate the initial point: Though I am about to explain why I don't think Scripture teaches that the Antichrist will be a Roman, I don't see any problem, theologically or otherwise, with that idea, and I would not be surprised if he did come from a European nation or coalition of nations.

Three places in Scripture are used to propose that the Antichrist will be Roman: Daniel 2:40–49, 7:7–28, and 9:26. While other passages reiterate that a tenfold leadership will be a part of the Antichrist's home kingdom, these are the only passages used to suggest that the ten-king nation or kingdom from which he comes will have characteristics of the ancient Roman Empire.

The first two passages, Daniel 2:40–49 and Daniel 7:7–28, should be considered a set since they are essentially combined to formulate the revived Roman Empire idea. At the heart of this teaching is a tradition that Daniel 2—which details a vision given to Nebuchadnezzar of a statue made of many metals that symbolize successive nations (Rome being the last of these)—is a mirror image of a vision given to Daniel in chapter 7, in which he sees four beasts coming out of the sea. The last beast Daniel sees in his vision is clearly the kingdom of the Antichrist. So proponents of this teaching reason that if the last empire in Nebuchadnezzar's dream is Rome, then the last beast that Daniel sees, which is clearly speaking of the Antichrist's kingdom, must be Rome as well. There is no indication in Scripture that we are supposed to assume that these two chapters are speaking of the same events; in fact, myriad reasons that strongly refute this idea are selectively overlooked by commentators. Many scholars with a wide range of prophetic opinions reject the notion of Daniel 2 and 7 describing the same thing. Some of these include G. H. Lang, Geoffrey R. King, David Pawson, Charles Cooper, Hanoch ben Keshet, Dr. Noah W. Hutchings, Dr. Henry M. Morris, and Irvin Baxter, Jr.

In addition to the argument that Daniel 2 and 7 are essentially the same, the revived Roman Empire idea is suggested because of what I believe is a misunderstanding of Daniel 2 regarding that last part of the last kingdom that Nebuchadnezzar sees in his dream (the feet, toes, and legs of iron).

Refuting these two ideas that have given us the concept of the revived Roman Empire will take some time. A detailed study of Daniel 2 and Daniel 7 is required to fully understand that this view is not taught in Scripture. However, including that study here would make this chapter more than thirteen thousand words long when the average word count per chapter is about four thousand words, I have included an exposition of those chapters in the appendix section of this book. If you are interested in such a study, I encourage you to check out the appendix now and come back to this chapter after you are finished.

The People of the Prince to Come

One other verse in Scripture is used to argue for a Roman Antichrist, and it is Daniel 9:26:

> And after the sixty-two weeks, an anointed one shall be cut off and shall have nothing. And the people of the prince who is to come shall destroy the city and the sanctuary. Its end shall come with a flood, and to the end there shall be war. Desolations are decreed.

In context, this verse is a prophecy of a destruction of the city of Jerusalem and the temple. It is almost universally believed to be a prophecy of the destruction of the city and temple by the Roman general Titus in AD 70. The word "prince" in the phrase "the people of the prince to come" is often taken to be speaking of the Antichrist; in other words: "There is a prince to come far in the future, but he won't be around at the time of the destruction of the temple in AD 70; only his *people* will, and *they* will destroy the temple." Therefore, this is often taken as a way to determine the nationality of the Antichrist. Most people who hold to this view see the Antichrist as Roman, since the Romans destroyed the temple in AD 70, and the verse says “the people of the prince who is to come shall destroy the city and the sanctuary.”

It should also be remembered that if indeed Daniel 2 or Daniel 7 isn’t speaking of a so-called revived Roman Empire, then this verse would be the only verse in the Bible that suggests a Roman nationality for the Antichrist.

I don’t think this verse is talking about the nationality of Antichrist—or anyone else’s nationality, for that matter—though it should be noted that I *do* think Antichrist is in view in the next verse. My opposition to the normal futurist interpretation is not because I am not a futurist—I obviously am—but it is only because I believe there is a much more logical explanation for this verse.

The phrase, “the people of the prince who is to come shall destroy the city and the sanctuary,” conveys what actually happened in AD 70. Not Titus, but his *people*—that is, the people under his command—destroyed the city and the temple. In almost any other sacking of any other city by the Romans, there would be no need to make this distinction. After all, if Titus or any other general ordered this to happen, he would be responsible for it, and Scripture would be right to put the blame on him. But the events of that day made it necessary for Scripture to describe the destruction of the temple and city as not being *by* Titus, but instead by his people.

According to Josephus, who was literally present and part of the court of Titus at the destruction of the city and temple, Titus did not order the temple destroyed. He had wanted to turn it into a temple for the Roman gods. But his people destroyed it anyway. It would be one thing if this were only briefly mentioned by Josephus, but instead, Josephus describes in many ways the moblike destruction of the temple and city despite Titus' repeated orders for the destruction to stop.

For example, Josephus quotes Titus in a meeting with his generals about what to do with the temple. This was because the Jews were using the temple as a citadel for a kind of last stand. Josephus says:

> But Titus said, that "although the Jews should get upon that holy house, and fight us thence, yet ought we not to revenge ourselves on things that are inanimate, instead of the men themselves;" and that he was not in any case for burning down so vast a work as that was, because this would be a mischief to the Romans themselves, as it would be an ornament to their government while it continued.

Then, after Titus was informed that, despite his orders, the soldiers set fire to the temple, Josephus describes the following scene:

> And now a certain person came running to Titus, and told him of this fire, as he was resting himself in his tent after the last battle; whereupon he rose up in great haste, and, as he was, ran to the holy house, in order to have a stop put to the fire.... Then did Caesar, both by calling to the soldiers that were fighting, with a loud voice, and by giving a signal to them with his right hand, order them to quench the fire. But they did not hear what he said, though he spake so loud, having their ears already dimmed by a greater noise another way; nor did they attend to the signal he made with his hand neither, as still some of them were distracted with fighting, and others with passion. But as for the legions that came running thither, neither any persuasions nor any threatenings could restrain their violence, but each one's own passion was his commander at this time.

Josephus offers still more descriptions of the events of that day:

> But as the flame had not as yet reached to its inward parts, but was still consuming the rooms that were about the holy house, and Titus supposing what the fact was, that the house itself might yet he saved, he came in haste and endeavored to persuade the soldiers to quench the fire, and gave order to Liberalius the centurion, and one of those spearmen that were about him, to beat the soldiers that were refractory with their staves, and to restrain them; yet were their passions too hard for the regards they had for Caesar, and the dread they had of him who forbade them, as was their hatred of the Jews, and a certain vehement inclination to fight them, too hard for them also.
>
> Moreover, the hope of plunder induced many to go on, as having this opinion, that all the places within were full of money, and as seeing that all round about it was made of gold.... And thus was the holy house burnt down, without Caesar's approbation.

If the Scripture had said that the prince—that is, Titus—destroyed the temple, it would have been factually inaccurate. Instead, it says "the *people of the prince*" destroyed it. I hope you can now see why this is an important distinction.

The "to come," as in "the people of the prince *who is to come*," is therefore from Daniel's perspective, as this prince (Titus) was almost five hundred years in the future at the time he wrote. But for us looking back, that prince to come has already come…and gone.

A note on the Hebrew word "prince": Though the word can mean "general," "leader," "king," or indeed a literal "prince," as in a "son of a king," it is interesting that at the time of the destruction of Jerusalem, Titus' father Vespasian was the emperor, making Titus a literal prince who would soon become emperor himself, as well as a general of an army. This means that Titus would fulfill every possible meaning for the Hebrew word "prince."

The argument against this idea would be that the next verse, which talks about the Antichrist, starts with the word "he." Those who would argue this point would say that the "he" must point back to the "prince" in the previous verse, but there are significant problems with that idea.

"Then **he** shall confirm a covenant with many for one week" (Daniel 9:27, emphasis added). There are really only two good possibilities from a grammatical perspective about the antecedent for the "he" in verse 27, though you likely will not hear either of them in a commentary on this passage. The possibilities offered in most commentaries will be first that the best antecedent for "he" is the "prince to come" of verse 26. This will be stated by the average futurist. And though I don't agree with the average futurists about the grammar here, it should be noted that I *do* agree with the reason they are trying to make this claim; that is because they think that this last verse is a future event and the person we will soon read about is the Antichrist.

The second possibility is that the antecedent for the "he" in verse 27 is the "anointed one" of verse 26, i.e., Jesus. This is usually put forth by preterists, and despite it being nearly impossible from a grammatical perspective, they put this forth because they believe that verse 27 is not a future event. It also puts the preterists in the precarious position of having to defend why Jesus would do the horrible things that the next few verses say this person does.

If we were to just consider this verse from a grammatical perspective, not a theological one, we would have to conclude that "people," as in the "people of the prince to come," is the antecedent for "he." Note the following quote from a study of this passage that brings out this point:

> With regards to the above Passage the subject noun is "People" (the ones destroying) and the parsed Hebrew word ישחית 7843 (ishchith-shachath) "He shall destroy" is used as a Hebrew hiphil, verb, imperfect, 3rd person, masculine, singular and, is completely acceptable in Hebrew with the use of the singular subject noun "People", whereas the translated word "People" in the above Passage is implied to be acting as a single unit—therefore a singular noun and, not a plural noun, receiving a 3ms verb.
>
> In addition, the Hebrew word "shachath" must also be translated as "He shall destroy" and not just simply as "shall destroy" unless the "HE" is either implied or articulated—written or verbally spoken because, the Hebrew word "shachath" is used in this Passage as a Hebrew hiphil, verb, imperfect, 3rd person, masculine, singular.
>
> Dan. 9:26 …and the people of the prince that shall come (He) shall destroy the city and the sanctuary…
>
> Therefore, if the subject noun in the above KJV, et. al., Passage is the singular "People" (and it indeed is) and it receives the corresponding 3rd ms verb "He shall destroy" then by legitimate Hebrew and English grammatical standards who must the "HE" of Dan. 9:27 be (and He shall confirm…)?

> Does consistent contiguous grammatical standards dictate that the "HE" of Dan. 9:27 be the same preceding antecedent singular subject noun "People" (the ones destroying) or can we just simply arbitrarily choose to substitute a different subject noun in the place of "people" – in this case the "a coming prince"?

The study concludes this way:

> Once again, any attempt then to "substitute" an alternate and arbitrary subject noun (*a coming prince*) for the *HE* of Dan. 9:27, even if we assume a theoretical gap, other than the clearly grammatically defined antecedent "*People*", the *HE* of Dan. 9:26, is to simply ignore all Hebrew and English grammatical rules merely to fit a theory.
>
> If we are going to go down that slippery slope where we ignore grammatical rules and standards simply to fit our theories then there is little hope of ever arriving at the truth of Scripture.[42]

In other words, if the "he" of verse 27 is supposed to look back at anything, it must look back to the "people." But the problem with that is that it makes no sense. This brings us to the last good possibility for the antecedent for the "he" of Daniel 9:27…

There is none.

I wrote former Moody Bible Institute professor Charles Cooper about this, and this was his response:

---

42 "How Can The 'HE' of Dan. 9:27 Be A Roman TYPE 'Coming Prince'", n.d. http://www.shalach.org/Antichrist/DAN-HE.htm.

> This is what I am convinced the text is actually intending. The "he" of verse 27 does not have an antecedent which drives scholars mad. They force the Hebrew to say something I don't believe it intended. The he of verse 27 does not look backwards, it points forward to a character not identified in the previous verses. This has caused [many problems]. It will continue.

I believe the "he" of verse 27 does speak of the Antichrist, so I have no reason to argue this point other than the fact that it is wrong to say the "prince to come" in verse 26 is also referring to the Antichrist. The "he" in verse 27 just comes out of nowhere. But, as I will suggest, we are given all the tools we will ever need to determine who the "he" is, because literally every aspect of the "he" here is described by Daniel in at least triplicate in other places in his writings when referring to the Antichrist.

Many futurists, including myself, have concluded that there is a gap of two thousand-plus years between the sixty-ninth and seventieth weeks of Daniel 9. I believe there is no other option but to see the sixty-ninth week ending at the second temple destruction and the last week beginning after another temple is built, an event that, as of July 2014, has not yet occurred. If this is true, then it also would explain the out-of-nowhere nature of the "he" at the beginning of verse 27. That is, it comes out of nowhere because the context of this verse is far removed from the previous verse, chronologically speaking. It's not as if the "he" would be unrecognized, though, as Daniel seems almost fixated on the Antichrist figure in Daniel 7, 8, 11, and 12, where he describes in detail the Antichrist's actions. So we are not left to guess as to who the "he" is in this verse.

In conclusion, only three passages in Scripture suggest that the Antichrist will be Roman. And while that idea is not harmful to the thesis of this book in the least, I feel that if we are to be the best watchmen we can be, we need to see that the modern interpretations of these three passages have serious problems, and there are much better, more hermeneutically consistent alternatives.

Chapter 9

Will the Antichrist Be an Assyrian?

A new and increasingly popular view is that the Antichrist will be an Assyrian. This conclusion is arrived at by a few passages in Isaiah, primarily Isaiah 10, and one passage in the book of Micah. I want to look closely at these passages as well as what the proponents of this view say about them to show you why I think this view is artificially contrived.

As in the case for the Roman Antichrist, even though I don't agree that the Bible makes this claim specifically, I don't necessarily have a problem with this idea theologically. I don't think the Bible is specific as to which ten-leader nation or coalition of nations the Antichrist comes from, and whether the Antichrist comes from Assyria or is ethically Assyrian makes little difference to the thesis of this book. The people making this claim, however, are using it to support the idea that the Antichrist will be committed to the religion of Islam—something I don't agree with. Even if the verses we are about to study were referring to an Assyrian Antichrist, which I strongly believe they are not, they still would not prove that the Antichrist was a religious Muslim.

With regard to the Islamic Antichrist view, I will be quoting extensively from Joel Richardson, who, I believe, is the most intelligent and articulate advocate for this view. I respect Mr. Richardson greatly, both as a fellow brother in Christ and as a researcher, and I hope my referencing his work on this will be seen as a compliment to him, because I consider his writings on the theory to be the best.

Isaiah

Let's first look at the passages used to support the Assyrian Antichrist view from the book of Isaiah. The context of Isaiah is extremely important for our discussion, so I will spend a few moments describing the issues the prophet was dealing with and writing about in his day.

Isaiah wrote when Israel was being threatened with destruction from the Assyrian king Sennacherib. Isaiah warns that this king, whom the prophet occasionally refers to as "the Assyrian," will capture and carry off the ten northern tribes, in addition to many cities in the Southern Kingdom, but that the city of Jerusalem would not fall and that God would come to His people's aid. All of this happens in the book: Sennacherib does indeed conquer the Northern Kingdom, as well as many cities in the Southern Kingdom. He even sets up a siege of the city of Jerusalem. But, as promised, God protects the city by sending an angel, who destroys 185,000 of the Assyrian soldiers surrounding the city and causes the rest of the army to flee, never to threaten Israel again. In addition to relating this judgment of Sennacherib, Isaiah also tells us that, later, the king himself is killed by his own sons. The Assyrian empire goes into sharp decline shortly after that and is eventually conquered by Neo-Babylon. The rest of the book of Isaiah is focused on warning Judah that although it was spared from the Assyrians, it would be captured by the empire that would come after the Assyrians: the Babylonians.

More than any other book, Isaiah is peppered with prophecies concerning the Messiah and the millennial reign. This is probably because Isaiah was giving the Northern and Southern Kingdoms terrible news: God had decreed that they both were going to be conquered, though at different times. So, the Lord made sure to include several references to the ultimate victory of the Jewish people in the kingdom of the Messiah. This pattern is seen throughout Scripture. Often, the most magnificent prophecies of Israel's future glory are given to Israel at a time when things look the most hopeless and they need the most encouragement. God wants Israel to know that, though things look bad at present, they will all work out in the end.

Since the book of Isaiah includes prophecies of the near future interwoven with prophecies of the distant future or "end times," there is much speculation as to which prophecies are which. Do the prophecies of the Assyrian have a near or distant fulfillment, or, as is so often the case in Scripture, is it a combination of both? While I agree totally with the concept of "types" of the Antichrist in Scripture, and even that Sennacherib is one of those types, a close look at the claims of Assyrian Antichrist proponents will make it clear that the prophecies of the Assyrian in Isaiah were never intended to give the reader any information about the nationality—let alone, the religion—of the Antichrist.

Joel Richardson, in his book, *Mideast Beast,* repeatedly tells his readers that the book of Isaiah says that the Messiah will defeat "the Assyrian":

> "God's promise was that a military leader would be born from the line of David who would deliver all of God's

> people from "the Assyrian." The problem, however, is that this never occurred in history."[43]
>
> "This passage declares that the Messiah will deliver Israel from the Assyrian."[44]
>
> "So despite the numerous references throughout Isaiah to the Messiah destroying the king of Assyria in the land of Israel, historically this deliverance never occurred."[45]

Richardson believes there are prophecies that say the Messiah will defeat "the Assyrian," and since this obviously has never happened, these passages must refer to the end times.

If there were such prophecies in Isaiah stating that the Messiah would defeat the Assyrian, I would have to agree with Richardson that there must be an Assyrian component to the Antichrist. But, as we will see, there isn't a single verse in all of Isaiah that says the Messiah will defeat the Assyrian; Richardson and others come to this conclusion in an extremely roundabout way.

The first thing that Richardson does to try to explain what he means by saying that the Messiah is said to destroy the Assyrian is point to Isaiah 7:14–20, which he uses to establish that there is a dual prophecy in certain sections of Isaiah that deal with the Assyrian. That passage begins with words that are familiar to Christians as partially a prophecy of Jesus' birth. But, as Richardson correctly points out, in the original context, these words are also a prophecy of a child in Isaiah's day who was to be a sign that the Assyrians were going to destroy much of Israel.

---

[43] Joel Richardson (2012-06-08). *Mideast Beast: The Scriptural Case for an Islamic Antichrist* (p. 235). Joel Richardson. Kindle Edition.

[44] Ibid., 238.

[45] Ibid., 239.

> Therefore the Lord Himself will give you a sign: Behold, the virgin shall conceive and bear a Son, and shall call His name Immanuel. Curds and honey He shall eat, that He may know to refuse the evil and choose the good. For before the Child shall know to refuse the evil and choose the good, the land that you dread will be forsaken by both her kings. The LORD will bring the king of Assyria upon you and your people and your father's house—days that have not come since the day that Ephraim departed from Judah.
>
> And it shall come to pass in that day
> That the LORD will whistle for the fly
> That is in the farthest part of the rivers of Egypt,
> And for the bee that is in the land of Assyria.
> They will come, and all of them will rest
> In the desolate valleys and in the clefts of the rocks,
> And on all thorns and in all pastures.
>
> In the same day the Lord will shave with a hired razor,
> With those from beyond the River, with the king of Assyria,
> The head and the hair of the legs,
> And will also remove the beard. (Isaiah 7:14–20)

The idea that this prophecy, in addition to being about the birth of Jesus, is also about a child as a sign of Israel's impending destruction is more clearly described in the next chapter.

> For before the child knows how to cry out, "My father" or "My mother," the wealth of Damascus and the plunder of Samaria will be carried off by the king of Assyria. (Isaiah 8:4)

Richardson wants to apply all of this prophecy, not just the virgin birth idea (7:14), to the Messiah in order to have a basis for saying that He will have some application to the Assyrian. There are a number of problems with this. The first is that, even if we allowed that every word of this prophecy was to be applied to Jesus in the end times, it still is not saying anything about the child defeating the Assyrian. In fact, it is quite clearly saying that the Assyrian empire will be victorious over the northern tribes. The child in this prophecy is doing nothing but acting as a sign that the destruction of Israel is imminent. There isn't a single aspect of this prophecy that gives the reader the idea that the child is to defeat the Assyrians. Yet, Richardson says of this passage that "the fuller context is the coming of the Messiah to break the Assyrian."[46] How can a prophecy that a child will be a sign of the destruction of Israel by the Assyrians be evidence that the child will destroy the Assyrians? The point of this passage is that the Assyrian armies are a judgment from God and they will be victorious, not defeated.

The second problem with this idea is that the destruction of the northern tribes of Israel is to occur before this child is able to talk (Isaiah 8:4). Obviously, there is danger in applying too much of this prophecy to Jesus, because there is nothing even remotely close to a fulfillment of this in the days after Jesus' birth. There was no attack from the long-dead Assyrian empire on the northern tribes before He was able to talk. Such a preposterous notion forces us to recognize what scholars have long known: The prophecy of the virgin birth In Isaiah 7:14, like so many other prophecies of the Messiah that have an original context, have a limit as to how much of that context we can apply to Jesus. For example, Matthew 2:14–15 states that when Joseph, Mary, and the infant Jesus came back to Israel from Egypt, where they had fled

[46] Ibid., 241.

to escape Herod, it was a fulfillment of Hosea 11:1, which says: "When Israel was a child, I loved him, And out of Egypt I called My son" (Hosea 11:1)

Here, the original context is speaking about Israel, but Matthew tells us it is also a picture of Jesus. We know to stop short at that verse and not apply the rest of Hosea 11 to Jesus, because the next verse begins: "As they called them, So they went from them; They sacrificed to the Baals, And burned incense to carved images" (Hosea 11:2).

So unless we are willing to say that Jesus made sacrifices to Baal, we would have to admit that there is a limit to how much of a messianic prophecy found in another context can apply to Jesus.

To conclude my main point on this: There is no mention of the Messiah defeating the Assyrian in Isaiah 7–8, no matter which way we look at it.

Let's move on to other evidence Richardson offers to support this most important claim that the Messiah is said to defeat the Assyrian. He quotes an obvious messianic prophecy in Isaiah 9:

> But there will be no gloom for her who was in anguish. In the former time he brought into contempt the land of Zebulun and the land of Naphtali, but in the latter time he has made glorious the way of the sea, the land beyond the Jordan, Galilee of the nations.
>
> The people who walked in darkness have seen a great light; those who dwelt in a land of deep darkness, on them has light shined.... For the yoke of his burden, and the staff for his shoulder, the rod of his oppressor, you have broken as on the day of Midian. For every boot of the tramping warrior in battle tumult and every garment rolled in blood

> will be burned as fuel for the fire. For to us a child is born, to us a son is given; and the government shall be upon his shoulder, and his name shall be called Wonderful Counselor, Mighty God, Everlasting Father, Prince of Peace. Of the increase of his government and of peace there will be no end, on the throne of David and over his kingdom, to establish it and to uphold it with justice and with righteousness from this time forth and forevermore. The zeal of the LORD of hosts will do this. (verses 1–7)

Richardson says, "This passage declares that the Messiah will deliver Israel from the Assyrian in the same manner that Gideon in Judges 8 delivered Israel from the Midianite armies."[47] That's quite a claim. Is this really telling us that Jesus will destroy the Assyrian? There is obviously no mention of the Assyrian or even Assyria in this passage. How is Richardson coming to this conclusion?

Before I answer that, let's consider this passage in context. As I have pointed out, it was pretty horrible news that the prophet Isaiah was told to deliver: God asked him to tell Israel that He was mad at them, and that He was going to send the Assyrians to wipe out the Northern Kingdom. The prophecy we just read tells of a future Israel in which the Messiah will rule with strength and justice. There will be no more conquering of Israel by its enemies when the Messiah begins His reign. This prophecy is clearly meant to be an encouragement to Israel in light of the fact that God is saying through Isaiah that it is about to be conquered.

Richardson essentially says that since this prophecy about hope for a future peace comes in close proximity to other chapters warning

---

[47] Ibid., 238.

of Israel's destruction by Assyria, *this is* a prophecy of the Messiah defeating Assyria when he comes, despite there being no mention whatsoever of the Messiah defeating Assyria. This same method of interpreting Scripture is also applied to Isaiah 10 in order to come to the Assyrian Antichrist view. Here how another author describes the basis for the idea that the Antichrist will be an Assyrian based on Isaiah 10:

> But there is a catch! Immediately after the Assyrian invades Israel in Isaiah chapter 10 we are introduced to the Messiah on earth! [in the next chapter] That is to say, Jesus Christ sets up his everlasting throne in Jerusalem. In other words this passage also predicts a future event. The Assyrian will once again invade Israel, and then Jesus Christ will come back to earth to defeat the Assyrian and to rule forever![48]

We can see from these words that the mere proximity of a chapter about the Assyrian to another chapter about the messianic kingdom is proof that the Messiah will destroy the Assyrian, despite no evidence in the text itself for such a scenario. This fits the definition of eisegesis (reading one's own ideas into the text).

There is simply no mention of the Messiah defeating the Assyrian in Isaiah 9:1–7, and there no evidence that this is the author's intent. If we were to apply this method of interpretation to other passages, we would have many contradictory proof texts for the origin of the Antichrist in Scripture. For example, later on in the book of Isaiah, when Assyria is out of the picture and Babylon is the main threat God is warning about, we find similar prophecies of hope in the future messianic kingdom directly after warnings of

---

[48] Craig C. White. "The Assyrian Is the Antichrist!", n.d. http://hightimetoawake.com/the-assyrian-is-the-antichrist/.

Judah's destruction by the king of Babylon. Are we to also assume that the Antichrist is a Babylonian? With only minor adjustments, using this method of interpretation, I could make a rock-solid case that the Antichrist must be an Egyptian. Warnings of various judgments followed by prophecies of the redemption of Israel is one of the most common motifs in the prophets' words. Unless the text offers a reason for us to think we are to apply wholesale the immediate context of the prophet to the prophecy of the Millennium that follows it, we shouldn't do it—unless we don't mind the myriad contradictions it creates.

The final section in Isaiah that Richardson appeals to is Isaiah 10. This is a chapter in which God tells His people that after He has used Sennacherib to destroy the Northern Kingdom and humble those in Jerusalem with famine, He will destroy Sennacherib as well. Then, after the Lord has finished His redeeming work of chastisement toward His people, He will punish the Assyrian: "When the Lord has finished all his work against Mount Zion and Jerusalem, he will say, 'I will punish the king of Assyria for the willful pride of his heart and the haughty look in his eyes'" (Isaiah 10:12).

The book of Isaiah gives us a picture of this judgment of the Assyrian twenty-six chapters later:

> Then the angel of the LORD went out, and killed in the camp of the Assyrians one hundred and eighty-five thousand; and when people arose early in the morning, there were the corpses—all dead. So Sennacherib king of Assyria departed and went away, returned home, and remained at Nineveh. Now it came to pass, as he was worshiping in the house of Nisroch his god, that his sons Adrammelech and Sharezer struck him down with the

> sword; and they escaped into the land of Ararat. Then Esarhaddon his son reigned in his place. (Isaiah 37:36–38)

Proponents of the Assyrian Antichrist view try to make the case that this judgment of Assyria is not yet complete. But, from a Biblical perspective, there is no doubt that the destruction of the 185,000 Assyrian soldiers and the murder of Sennacherib by his sons, as well as the eventual desolation of the Assyrian empire are considered God's judgment against "the Assyrian," because Jeremiah refers to God's judgment of the Assyrian as a past-tense event in his day: "Therefore thus says the LORD of hosts, the God of Israel: 'Behold, I will punish the king of Babylon and his land, **As I have punished the king of Assyria'"**– (Jeremiah 50:18, emphasis added).

Richardson makes the case that, despite Jeremiah and Ezekiel saying that the judgment of the king of Assyria in Isaiah 10 is complete, it can't be fulfilled, because Isaiah 14 says: "I will break the Assyrian **in My land**, And on My mountains tread him underfoot. Then his yoke shall be removed from them, And his burden removed from their shoulders" (Isaiah 14:25).

He says that since Sennacherib wasn't killed in Israel, but back home in Assyria by his sons, there must be a future fulfillment in which some other Assyrian man is killed, but this time in Jerusalem. This is answered with a simple study of the grammar of the passage. This is not a reference to the king of Assyria being "broken," but rather to the fact that the "burden" of the Assyrian yoke was forever broken on the day that God killed 185,000 Assyrians and they left Israel for good. The NET Bible translates the passage this way: "I will break **Assyria** in my land, I will trample **them** underfoot on my hills. **Their** yoke will be removed from my people, the burden will be lifted from their shoulders" (Isaiah 14:25, emphasis added).

The endnotes explain that the pronouns are collective singular, meaning they likely refer to the nation and not the king. The actual Hebrew word sometimes translated "the Assyrian" is simply "Ashshuwr," which is ambiguous because it can mean Assyria or Assyrian. So this is not a reason to deny that God has not fulfilled His judgment on that nation or that king. It should also be noted that the prophecies of Assyria's past-tense judgment are spoken of in Ezekiel 31: 3–17, which reiterates the very elements described in Isaiah 10. The fact is that shortly after this prophecy of the destruction of Assyria was given, its capital, Nineveh, the largest city on earth at the time, became a desolate wasteland, fulfilling precisely what God said He would do; there is no reason to say that He is waiting to do it again.

Richardson also asserts that Isaiah 14 proves that the destruction of Assyria must be in the future, because it says that Assyria's yoke will be removed from Israel when God judges it. Richardson makes the case that since the Babylonians who came after the Assyrians controlled Israel as well, the yoke was never really removed. Again, he is reading too much into the text. Isaiah 14:25 isn't saying that all yokes that have ever been or will ever be will be removed when He destroys Assyria; it only indicates that the Assyrian yoke will be removed. This seems to be quite clear from the phrase "**their** yoke will be removed from my people" in reference to the Assyrians.

We have seen that there is absolutely no reference in the book of Isaiah to the Messiah defeating the Assyrian; there are only references to Assyria being used by God to destroy Israel, and then to God destroying Assyria when He is through with it, which He did in glorious fashion. We have also seen that most of the ways people force the idea of the Messiah defeating someone called the Assyrian in the end times is by pointing out that certain messianic prophecies appear in close proximity to chapters about Assyria.

We have also seen that the references to "the Assyrian" in the book are references to Sennacherib, references that do not require a future double fulfillment.

Micah 5:5

Micah 5:5 provides the best hope for anyone wanting to say the Antichrist is an Assyrian, in my opinion. But, as I plan to show, it is a false hope. It is no surprise that Micah mentions "the Assyrian," since he wrote at the exact same time as Isaiah, during the period when Assyria was threatening Israel. Sennacherib was public enemy number one in his day, and this fact is evident throughout his writings.

The passage in question is another prophecy of the Millennium, another encouragement to the people of Israel that one day they would not have to deal with being continually conquered, a day when the Messiah would rule Israel with an iron rod. The difference between this passage and the others we looked at in Isaiah is that Micah actually mentions the phrase "the Assyrian" within the millennial context. In other words, the phrase "the Assyrian" is not just *near* a chapter about the Messiah; it's actually *in* the same chapter and context, therefore, it gives us a much better reason to consider whether we should expect an Assyrian in an end-times context. The passage reads:

> But you, Bethlehem Ephrathah,
> Though you are little among the thousands of Judah,
> Yet out of you shall come forth to Me
> The One to be Ruler in Israel,
> Whose goings forth are from of old,
> From everlasting.

Therefore He shall give them up,
Until the time that she who is in labor has given birth;
Then the remnant of His brethren
Shall return to the children of Israel.
And He shall stand and feed His flock
In the strength of the LORD,
In the majesty of the name of the LORD His God;
And they shall abide,
For now He shall be great
To the ends of the earth;
And this One shall be peace.

When the Assyrian comes into our land,
And when he treads in our palaces,
Then we will raise against him
Seven shepherds and eight princely men.
They shall waste with the sword the land of Assyria,
And the land of Nimrod at its entrances;
Thus He shall deliver us from the Assyrian,
When he comes into our land
And when he treads within our borders.

Then the remnant of Jacob
Shall be in the midst of many peoples,
Like dew from the LORD,
Like showers on the grass,
That tarry for no man
Nor wait for the sons of men.
And the remnant of Jacob
Shall be among the Gentiles,
In the midst of many peoples,
Like a lion among the beasts of the forest,
Like a young lion among flocks of sheep,
Who, if he passes through,

> Both treads down and tears in pieces,
> And none can deliver.
> Your hand shall be lifted against your adversaries,
> And all your enemies shall be cut off. (Micah 5:2–9, NKJV, emphasis added)

The Assyrian Antichrist proponents would say that the fact that Micah mentioned the Assyrian in the context of the Millennium is clearly proof that Messiah will defeat “the Assyrian” in the end times, and that the Antichrist is an Assyrian.

However, there are quite a few problems with this interpretation, the first being that it is almost certainly not Micah’s intention to give a prophecy of a future attack of an Assyrian in the Millennium. Rather, he is essentially saying, “Yes, it’s really terrible for us right now, being attacked by the Assyrians, but keep in mind that when the Messiah comes, everything will be different. And **should** the Assyrians **try** to invade our land at that time, we would totally prevail over them.” This interpretation is not wishful thinking on my part. The NET Bible translation of this passage highlights Micah’s *hypothetical* intention:

> He will give us peace.
> **Should** the Assyrians **try** to invade our land
> and attempt to set foot in our fortresses,
> we will send against them seven shepherd-rulers,
> make that eight commanders.
> They will rule the land of Assyria with the sword,
> the land of Nimrod with a drawn sword.
> Our king will rescue us from the Assyrians
> **should they attempt** to invade our land

> and try to set foot in our territory. (Micah 5:5–6,[49] emphasis added)

The reason Micah, through the inspiration of the Holy Spirit, uses the Assyrians as an example of people who wouldn't be able to attack Israel when the Messiah comes is tied to the reason this message of hope was given in the first place. The people of Israel were being so terribly destroyed by the Assyrians, it seemed that the promises of God would never come true. It would be like saying to the Jews in Nazi Germany: "In the Kingdom Age, if Hitler tries to harm us, we will defeat him with the help of the Messiah."

Another massive problem for the Assyrian Antichrist proponent using Micah 5:5 is that this is clearly a reference to events within the millennial reign itself, which would preclude this having anything to do with the Antichrist, who is thrown into the lake of fire never to come out again (Revelation 19:20, 20:10). The Antichrist's destruction occurs *before* the Millennium even begins, making it impossible for this to refer to the Antichrist. By contrast, Satan is thrown into the "bottomless pit" at the beginning of the Millennium, and is let out at the end for one last deception, in which he gathers people and nations to march on the beloved city in a very unsuccessful campaign. But, after that, he is thrown into the lake of fire, the place where the Antichrist has apparently been the whole time (Revelation 20:1–10, 19:20). If we absolutely had to link the reference to an Assyrian in Micah 5:5 to a future event, we would be limited to it being a reference to Satan or one of the people he recruits to march on Jerusalem at the end of the Millennium. There is no theological scenario that allows for the

[49] Biblical Studies Press. (2006). The NET Bible First Edition; Bible. English. (Micah 5:5–6).

Antichrist to cause problems during the Millennium; and therefore, there is no possibility that the Assyrian in Micah 5:5 refers to the Antichrist.

This concludes our study on the references to the Assyrian in Isaiah and Micah. I hope that I have presented some reasons to doubt the recent theory that Scripture teaches that the Antichrist will be an Assyrian.

Chapter 10

Will the Antichrist Claim to Be Jesus?

The question of whether the Antichrist will claim to be Jesus is more difficult than we might think. However, a number of passages might help us come to an answer. In the Olivet Discourse, Jesus warns His followers about "false christs" on a few occasions; for example, Matthew 24:24 says that "false christs and false prophets will rise and show great signs and wonders to deceive, if possible, even the elect."

Here we are warned of false christs. I would remind the reader that the word "christ" simply means "messiah"; it doesn't necessarily refer to Jesus. So, it is difficult to determine if any of these christs will claim to be Jesus based on the use of this word alone. It could be referring to someone claiming to be the Messiah to the Jews, or it could indicate someone claiming to be Jesus.

The plural "christs" is interesting here, because in another verse in the same chapter, Jesus makes it clear that "many" of these false christs will come. I take these references to many false messiahs to mean that the end times will be marked by great messianic expectations. Messianic fervor, and with it messianic pretenders, always have arisen when during significant Jewish events in history. For example, of the twenty-five or so false Jewish messiahs who have arisen over the centuries, most were piggybacking on noteworthy events in Jewish history, when expectations of deliverance or victory were very high. The end times, as I understand them, will be nothing if not a series of significant events for Israel. So the fact that many false messiahs will put their hats into the ring during that time is to be expected.

It is clear that although Jesus warns of multiple false christs, He intends the reader to understand that one of these false messiahs stands alone as the main one—that is, the Antichrist—and that these warnings also apply to the Antichrist. Of all the warnings Jesus gives in this chapter, He spends the most time describing the danger of the "abomination of desolation" spoken of by Daniel the prophet "standing in the Holy Place" (Matthew 24:15), where only the Antichrist is in view. Paul explains and expands on this particular teaching of Jesus in 2 Thessalonians: 2–11, which is one of the most detailed descriptions of the doctrine of the Antichrist in Scripture describing in great detail this man's actions: sitting in the temple declaring himself to be God, etc. In addition, Jesus mentions the false christs and false prophets showing "great signs and wonders to deceive," a phrase Paul attributes to the "lawless one" in 2 Thessalonians 2:9, seeming to suggest that Paul saw Jesus' warnings about the false messiahs to directly apply to the Antichrist. So there is a solid basis to believe that these phrases about the many false christs also pertain to the main and final False Messiah, the Antichrist.

One verse that seems to suggest the Antichrist will claim to be Jesus is found in Matthew 24:5: "For many will come in My name, saying, 'I am the Christ,' and will deceive many."

In parallel passages of this verse, like Mark 13:6, some translations use the words, "For many will come in My name, saying **I am he,**" instead of "I am the Messiah," but it should be noted that the original Greek does not contain the word "he," and it often appears in italics because it is an addition of the translators. The NET Bible includes a footnote after the "I am he" phrase, which says: "That is, 'I am the Messiah.'"

The first part of this verse, "For many will come in My name," seems to suggest that many of the false christs will claim to be Jesus because of the phrase "in My name," though the second part of the verse, which gives us an example of what they will say, "I am the Christ," leaves the matter open to debate, in my opinion. Is Jesus saying that the "many" will use His name specifically, or is He using the phrase "in My name" in the way that it is used in other places, to say that the they will be claiming His rightful title or authority?

One of the reasons I'm not too quick to say that this verse means that the Antichrist will claim to be Jesus is because of the use of a similar phrase in a similar context found in John chapter 5: "I have come in My Father's name, and you do not receive Me; if another comes in his own name, him you will receive" (John 5:43).

This says the Antichrist will come in his *own name,* which seems to contradict the idea that he comes in Jesus' name in Matthew 24:5. A resolution could be that in this verse, coming in someone's "name" refers to coming to do that person's will, as opposed to that person calling himself by that name. Jesus, in the chapter where we find this verse, makes it clear that He has come to do His Father's will (John 5:19, 30, 36), which is why He says He has come in His *Father's* name; whereas the Antichrist, who is sometimes called the "willful king," is said many times to do his *own* will (Daniel 11:16, 36). This is why Jesus says He comes in His *own name*. In Matthew 24:5, coming in Jesus' name must mean something different, however, because we know that the false messiahs are not coming to do Jesus' will, although they are said to come in His name. If this is true, it would be good evidence that the Antichrist will claim to be Jesus.

One of the reasons I lean toward the view that the Antichrist will in some way or another claim to be Jesus is because of Matthew 24:23–27, which says:

> Then if anyone says to you, "Look, here is the Christ!" or "There!" do not believe it. For false christs and false prophets will rise and show great signs and wonders to deceive, if possible, even the elect. See, I have told you beforehand. Therefore if they say to you, "Look, He is in the desert!" do not go out; or "Look, He is in the inner rooms!" do not believe it. For as the lightning comes from the east and flashes to the west, so also will the coming of the Son of Man be.

This was spoken to people who were followers of Christ and understood that there would be a *second* coming of Christ. After all, disciples' question cited at the beginning of this chapter was, "What will be the *sign of Your coming*, and of the end of the age?" It seems to me that Jesus is warning His followers about false messiahs who are claiming to fulfill the second coming of Christ, which means the people He is warning them about, who are in the desert or inner rooms, must also be claiming to be Jesus, if they want believers to think the second coming has occurred. Jesus says these weak attempts at a second coming will not be true, because *His* coming will be as "the lightning comes from the east and flashes to the west." In other words, it will not be something that will be easily mistaken or missed. So, because Jesus seems intent on warning Christians about false messiahs claiming to be carrying out the second coming of Jesus, a first coming is presupposed, and these people necessarily must be claiming to be the return of Jesus.

If it is true that the Antichrist intends to deceive Christians into thinking that he is the second coming of Jesus, then that whole scenario will depend on either an ignorance of Scripture or a willingness on the part of professing Christians to minimize Scripture. I say this because the Antichrist is said to come on the scene as either a political or military leader from a place with ten kings or kingdoms. He presumably rises in the ranks and has a very earthly, though tremendously successful, kingdom. It is absurd for a Bible-believing Christian to think the second coming of Christ will be so mundane. The idea that His return will occur by rising in the ranks of some earthly kingdom as a political or military leader as opposed to a sudden and glorious appearance in the clouds with angels is just not possible unless one is willing to seriously allegorize and minimize the Scriptures, which state so clearly that His coming will be glorious and unmistakable. However, Jesus' warnings in this passage seem to be against just such an error. He essentially says not to be fooled: "My coming will not be so obscure."

Let's explore some of the implications and questions that arise from the view that this false Jewish messiah will also claim to be Jesus. The first thing that comes to mind is how much more powerful this deception would be for professing Christians who would see the Antichrist, who would be claiming to be the return of Christ, miraculously conquer and subdue the Muslim world and set up a lookalike millennial kingdom. It would give new meaning to the warnings Jesus gave to His followers about the power of the end-times deception of the elect.[50] The only thing that would prevent Christians from believing this lie, other than the Holy Spirit, would be a solid knowledge of the Scriptures. As we have seen, although the Antichrist will do a pretty good job of looking as if he is fulfilling the Scriptures concerning the return of Christ and the setting up of a millennial kingdom, there are numerous things that he won't be able to do. For example, he almost

[50] Matthew 24:4, 24.

certainly will not build the millennial temple Ezekiel describes, which is larger than the entire city of Jerusalem, nor will he be able to make a new heavens and new earth. I doubt lions will lay down with lambs under his reign, either.

This brings us to an important point: If the Antichrist does claim to be Jesus, he will be a much different Jesus, with a very different doctrine. As I have said, he must minimize the Scriptures to a large degree, perhaps even forbidding the reading of the New Testament, claiming it has been perverted, just like so many cult leaders before him. Though we can only get glimpses of the Antichrist's doctrine, no matter which way we look at it, he will be teaching a perverted version of the Scriptures. We can only guess about the specifics of those teachings; unfortunately, we must wait to see.

Moving on to the Jewish view of the Messiah, it is very difficult to see how a man claiming to be Jesus could be embraced by the Jewish people who currently reject Jesus with such a passion. I am reminded of a quote from Rabbi Elaine Rose Glickman, who, in the book, *The Messiah and the Jews: Three Thousand Years of Tradition, Belief and Hope,* answers the question of how Jewish people will keep from falling for another false messiah:

> We will know [who the Messiah is], Judaism counsels, as long as we seek redemption rather than a redeemer. After all, anyone can claim to be our redeemer, and many have. But not even the most successful Messianic pretenders were able to achieve redemption. It is so simple, and yet so clear and true: we will recognize the Messiah not because of the way he looks, not because of a forceful personality

> or esoteric origin, but because he will accomplish the Messianic tasks.[51]

Glickman defines those Messianic tasks as the "revival of the temple in Jerusalem" and the "triumph of Israel over enemies who sought her destruction." So, it may be that if the Antichrist can offer these things, which Scripture says he will do, they will be willing to accept him, even if he claims to be Jesus.

Even though I favor the idea that the Antichrist will claim to be Jesus in some way, even a perverted version, I don't consider any of the verses we have studied in this chapter conclusive enough to become dogmatic about the point. We need to be prepared to see a false messiah who blasphemes Jesus and claims that He wasn't the fulfillment of the Scriptures, as well as a false messiah who claims to be the returning Jesus.

---

51 Rabbi Elaine Rose Glickman, (2013-02-21). *The Messiah and the Jews: Three Thousand Years of Tradition, Belief and Hope* (Kindle Locations 615-624). Jewish Lights Publishing. Kindle Edition.

Chapter 11

The Gog-Magog War Part 1: Intro and Timing

Over the centuries, Christians, Jews, and Muslims have wondered about the meaning and timing of Ezekiel 38 and 39, which contain a prophecy about a future war in which many nations march against Israel but are miraculously destroyed by God. There have been a multitude of interpretations of when this event will happen and which nations will be involved. Within Christianity alone, every generation of the church has applied this prophecy to its own time. For example, before the fall of the Roman Empire, church fathers like Eusebius wrote that the two Ezekiel chapters were a reference to the Romans. After the fall of Rome, other church fathers like Ambrose wrote that the passages were referring to the invading Goths, noting the "similarity of the last syllable" (of "Magog" and "Goths"). After the Goths, it was Attila and the Huns, then the Mongols, the Celts, the Khazars, the European Jews, and the Ottoman Turks. During the Cold War, it was Russia, a view promoted by Hal Lindsey in his book, *The Late Great Planet Earth*, and after 9/11, it is often seen as a reference to Islamic countries.

I believe that understanding the Gog and Magog war in Ezekiel 38 and 39 is important when trying to understand the end times in general, but I also believe the Antichrist will exploit the often-wrong views of Christians, Jews, and Muslims about the Gog-Magog war to great advantage during his rise to power—a view I will explain in a later chapter. In this chapter, I intend to show that there isn't any reason for this issue to be so confusing to Christians, because the relevant texts provide all the information we need to determine, at the very least, the timing of the war, which I believe is the most important element. I will begin by discussing many of the modern views on Gog-Magog and by looking at their strengths and weaknesses. I will then lay out a case for my own view, as well as anticipate criticism of it.

Different Views

Though I will not list the strengths and weaknesses of the Jewish and Islamic views about the Gog-Magog war, I will begin this section with a description of their views in order for the reader to understand that these religions also have many of the same difficulties with its interpretation, and also to show that all three of the Abrahamic religions are anticipating the Gog-Magog war.

The Jewish View

Just like the Christians, over the years, the Jews have interpreted this prophecy in light of their contemporary history. For example, the enemies in the Gog and Magog war were often seen by Jews as the Christians, Muslims, or both during times of Jewish persecution. Gog was seen as referring to Napoleon during the Napoleonic wars, and during both world wars, each was seen as the fulfillment of Ezekiel 38 and 39. Like Christians, Jews have also been quite divided about the timing of this war. For some, the Gog-Magog war is simply representative of past struggles; for others, the war of Gog occurs in the future, during the time of Messiah ben Joseph (the battle in which he is killed) but before the reign of Messiah ben David. Still others, including many of Judaism's most celebrated ancient writers like Saadia,

Maimonides, and Nahmanides, wrote that the Gog-Magog war would occur after Messiah ben David, the final Messiah, had been ruling over a restored Israel for some time, in what Christians call the Millennium.

The Islamic View

Gog and Magog are referred to in Arabic as Ya'juj and Ma'juj. The war they start is the fifth "Major sign" in Islamic eschatology. Although they are sometimes individuals, sometimes peoples, and sometimes geographical regions, the references to them in the Quran and hadiths clearly indicate that Gog and Magog are people who are numerous in number who will appear toward the end times. One hadith says the following about the ethnicity and appearance of the people involved: "Gog and Magog belong to the Turkic Mongol race, have small eyes, small flat noses and wide faces. Their faces look like hammered-out shields."

The Muslims believe this war happens after the Mahdi and Isa have appeared and defeated the Dajjal (the Islamic Antichrist). They say that after Isa has killed, or converted everyone to Islam, Allah lets Gog and Magog out from the behind a wall where they are held at bay. Gog and Magog then kill almost everyone on the earth; in fact, even Isa and his followers need to flee to a stronghold in Sinai for safety. After some time, Isa prays to Allah, who sends a bird that drops a worm into the necks of these armies, which causes all of the soldiers to die in one night. There is much less speculation in Islam regarding the timing of this event, probably because in this view, the Gog-Magog war has to be preceded by the appearance of the Mahdi and Isa and the destruction of the Dajjal, which are all events that would be quite obvious if they occurred.

Christian Views

The Christian views about the timing of the Gog-Magog war are divided into four categories:

1. Pre-Seventieth Week of Daniel
2. Mid-Seventieth Week of Daniel
3. Armageddon
4. End of the Millennium

Though there are subsets for most of these categories—for example, at least two views of the timing of the war fall under the umbrella of "pre-seventieth week of Daniel"—I'm limiting this discussion to these four broad categories, as the problems with the main category applies to all of its subsets as well.

Pre-Seventieth Week of Daniel

The problems with viewing the Gog-Magog war as occurring before the seventieth week of Daniel begins are as follows:

1) Ezekiel 39:7 says Yahweh's name is never to be profaned again after the end of the Gog-Magog war:

> So I will make My holy name known in the midst of My people Israel, and I will not let them profane My holy name anymore. Then the nations shall know that I am the LORD, the Holy One in Israel. (Ezekiel 39:7)

The seventieth week of Daniel, the time of the Antichrist, is characterized by blasphemy and rebellion against God, both on the part of the Antichrist, who is particularly blasphemous, and those who follow him. For example, Scripture says that people will "blaspheme the God of heaven because of their pains and their sores" (also see Revelation 17:3, 13:6, and 16:9–11).

The people in Israel rejoice at the deaths of the two witnesses (Revelation 11:10), which doesn't sound to me like people who are finished with rebellion against God. If the Gog-Magog war occurs before the seventieth week of Daniel, then we need to explain how the blasphemy and rebellion by the Antichrist and the people of the earth in the end times do not constitute a defiling of God's name. This problem is insurmountable, in my opinion.

2) The nations recognize the sovereignty of God as a result of the Gog-Magog war:

> I will bring you against my land so that the nations may acknowledge me, when before their eyes I magnify myself. (Ezekiel 38:16b)
>
> I will exalt and magnify myself; I will reveal myself before many nations. Then they will know that I am the LORD. (Ezekiel 38:23)
>
> Then the nations will know that I am the LORD, the Holy One of Israel. (Ezekiel 39:7b)

The nations are explicitly in rebellion against God throughout the seventieth week of Daniel (Revelation 11:2, 18:3, and 16:14). In fact, it seems that the "kings of the earth" who are gathered to battle against Christ at Armageddon include all or most of the nations of the earth. So we would need to explain how this contradiction is reconciled.

3) Israel also recognizes the Lord's sovereignty in totality (Northern and Southern Kingdoms) after Gog-Magog:

> So the house of Israel shall know that I am the LORD their God from that day forward. (Ezekiel 39:22)

The salvation of Israel en masse cannot happen before the conclusion of the seventieth week of Daniel. In fact the whole point of the seventieth-week prophecy is that the entirety of the seventy weeks (including the last seven years) needs to be completed before the salvation of Israel will occur:

> Seventy weeks are determined
> For your people and for your holy city,
> To finish the transgression,
> To make an end of sins,
> To make reconciliation for iniquity,
> To bring in everlasting righteousness,
> To seal up vision and prophecy,
> And to anoint the Most Holy. (Daniel 9:24)

This also violates the purpose of the "time of Jacob's trouble," which is a purifying event for the Jews during the last half of the final seven-year period culminating in their repentance and recognition of God. They will not be completely saved until after this purification event is completed.

4) Phrases like "dwelling securely," "dwelling in a land that has undergone a restoration from the sword," "a land of unwalled villages," "peaceful people, who dwell safely, all of them dwelling without walls, and having neither bars nor gates" are all inconsistent with Israel's geopolitical situation currently or for the foreseeable future. Nor could one argue that this is some kind of false security brokered by the Antichrist, since that event isn't supposed to occur until the first day of the seventieth week.

Mid-Seventieth Week of Daniel

Those who hold to the view that the Gog-Magog war occurs sometime in the midst of the seventieth week of Daniel usually see the abomination of desolation, which occurs at the midpoint, as the time when Israel comes to know God. They see references to "dwelling peacefully" and "without walls" explained by the false peace of the Antichrist during the first three and a half years of Daniel's seventieth week. A number of different scenarios proposed place the Gog-Magog war within the seventieth week, all of which suffer from similar problems:

1) There is no indication that after the Gog-Magog war, Israel will once again be subjected to conquest, which would necessarily be the case if it occurred at the midpoint, since a great deal of destruction and conquest begins at that time (Matthew 24:15–21). Ezekiel says that there will be no one to "make them afraid" and that God will leave "none of them captive any longer" after the war. This view essentially has Israel being miraculously delivered by God, only to be handed over to the Antichrist again for the final part of the seventieth week. Zechariah 13:8–9 says that two-thirds of Israel will be killed during this time, and Revelation 11:2 says the Gentiles will trample Jerusalem for three and a half years after this point. This is hardly consistent with the language of a final victory and establishment of universal peace that seem to come after the Gog-Magog war.

2) Israel is said to bury bodies for seven months and use the weapons of the dead soldiers for fuel for seven years after the Gog-Magog war. This is inconceivable during the great Tribulation, when the saints are hunted and killed, and the trumpet and bowl judgments take place.

3) Related to the previous point, the burying of bodies is described in Ezekiel 39 as a triumphant event that cleanses the land:

> For seven months the house of Israel will be burying them, in order to cleanse the land. Indeed all the people of the

> land will be burying, and they will gain renown for it on the day that I am glorified," says the Lord GOD. (Ezekiel 39:12–13)

How can the land be considered cleansed or even begging to be cleansed during a time before the final judgments found in Revelation, which, for example, turn the sea into blood and kill all life in the sea? A plain reading of Ezekiel 38–39 is a picture of a final destruction, which is followed by restoration, but this view anticipates that the Gog-Magog war is followed by the worst persecutions and devastation the world has ever seen.

4) This view presumes that phrases like "dwelling securely" or "a peaceful people, who dwell safely, all of them dwelling without walls, and having neither bars nor gates" refer to a false peace given by the Antichrist at the beginning of the seven-year period. This is a classic example of reading one's preconceived notions into the text. I don't think anyone who holds to this view would disagree with the fact that there is absolutely no suggestion in Ezekiel 38–39 that this is a false peace; the idea must be read back into the text. Not one word in these chapters would give the reader the notion that this peace is from anyone else but God and that it will be anything but everlasting. Indeed, the destruction of Gog-Magog seems to only prove that the original peace is in fact genuine, since the armies are destroyed by God before they even have a chance to attack.

There has been a good deal of scholarly work showing that the specific phrases used by Ezekiel to describe the peace are phrases that are used elsewhere to describe the millennial peace. Ralph H. Alexander has said the following in his paper, "A Fresh Look at Ezekiel 38 and 39":

> The expression "in the last days" (be'aharit hayyamim), found in Ezekiel 38:16, places these events at the end time, for this phrase is most frequently employed to designate the time of Israel's final restoration to the land and the period of Messiah's rule (cf. Isa. 2:2; Jer. 23:20; 30:24; Hosea 3:5; Mic. 4:1; Dan. 10:14).... Another significant factor in these chapters is the employment of the expression "living securely" (a form of yasab followed by labetah) in Ezekiel 38:8, 11, 14 and Ezekiel 39:26. This phrase is often employed in reference to millennial security, especially in Jeremiah and Ezekiel (cf. Jer. 23:6; 32:27; Ezek. 28:26; Zech. 14:11). This expression is used previously by Ezekiel in this series of messages to describe a definitely millennial picture (Ezek. 34:25-28; cf. Mic. 4:4).... These chronological notices in Ezekiel 38 and 39, in conjunction with the temporal *emphasis of the entire context of* these six night messages, argues strongly that the events of Ezekiel 38 and 39 transpire at the end time when Israel has already been restored to the land, the Messiah is present, and she has entered into the Peace covenant with Yahweh her Lord.

The mid-seventieth-week view also suffers from the problems of the pre-seventieth-week view, namely, that Yahweh's name will be profaned again, and the subjection of the nations and Israel cannot occur until the end of the seventieth week.

Armageddon

The view that the Gog Magog war is essentially the same war as the battle of Armageddon has much more credibility than the ones we have looked at thus far, though it also has problems. This view does seem more consistent with Ezekiel 38–39 in that it, too, is a final battle followed by peace and not continual war or persecution. The general scope of the event is more or less the same as well: Armies are gathered, then they are destroyed supernaturally, leaving behind a multitude of dead bodies. There is even a reference to the birds feasting on dead bodies in both passages. There are much fewer problems with this view, but the main problem it does have is devastating, in my opinion.

The idea that Israel would be "dwelling securely" in the way described by Ezekiel just before the battle of Armageddon is absurd. As mentioned previously, if there was ever a time that Israel is *not* dwelling in peace, it would be the time of just before Armageddon, when there is no more grass, clean water, or fish in the sea. This is a time when the Antichrist's persecution is at its height, when all those who do not worship the beast are killed, and when Jerusalem has been trampled by the Gentiles for the last three and a half years.

But because there is so much in common between Armageddon and Ezekiel 38 and 39, I hesitate to do away with it altogether, and I think it is possible that it is to be seen as a near or type fulfillment of the Gog-Magog war, with the ultimate and most literal fulfillment being the next view we will cover.

End of the Millennium

The view that the Gog-Magog war occurs after the end of the millennial reign, when Satan is let out to gather nations to battle Jerusalem but is defeated by God, is the only view on the timing of this war that enjoys explicit biblical support. It is the only view that has no inherent contradictions and makes sense of the entire prophecy of Ezekiel that begins in chapter 33 and continues through chapter 39. The arguments leveled against it are often superficial and will be dealt with at length at the end of this chapter.

Let me start by explaining what I mean when I say that this view enjoys explicit biblical support in regards to the timing of the war. In Revelation 20, the apostle John states when the battle of Gog and Magog will occur:

> **Now when the thousand years have expired**, Satan will be released from his prison and will go out to deceive the nations which are in the four corners of the earth, **Gog and Magog**, to gather them together to battle, whose number is as the sand of the sea. They went up on the breadth of the earth and surrounded the camp of the saints and the beloved city. And fire came down from God out of heaven and devoured them. The devil, who deceived them, was cast into the lake of fire and brimstone where the beast and the false prophet are. And they will be tormented day and night forever and ever. (Revelation 20:7–10, emphasis added)

John says this event will occur when the "thousand years have expired"—after the Millennium, after Jesus has been ruling on earth during an unprecedented time of peace. John uses the exact phrase "Gog and Magog," a phrase used only one other time—in Ezekiel 38–39—and the details of the battle John describes is consistent with what is described by Ezekiel, though obviously an abbreviated version. Ralph Alexander says of this reference to Gog-Magog:

> The strong basis for this position is the explicit reference to Gog and Magog in Revelation 20:8. Such an explicit reference cannot be dismissed lightly, as is often the case. The terms employed in Revelation 20:8 are the same as

> those in Ezekiel 38 and 39. Normal hermeneutics would require the identification of the two passages (since the terms Gog and Magog are used nowhere else in the Scriptures) unless strong reasons can be brought forth to deny such an equation.

It is so frustrating to hear commentators and preachers speak about this passage and dismiss it with a wave of their hands, because the excuses they give for its dismissal are not at all convincing, and sometimes even misleading. For example, they almost always say something similar to this: "The armies in Ezekiel come from the north; but in Revelation 20 the armies come from the 'four corners of the earth.'" This objection is easily dealt with by noting that in Ezekiel 38:5, 6 ,13 and 39:6, nations from all the compass points are specifically mentioned: Persia from the east, Cush (Ethiopia) from the south, Put (Libya) and the people who dwell "carelessly in the isles" from the west, and Gomer and Togarmah from the north. Why they insist that the armies in Ezekiel only come from the north is beyond me.

Some argue that the term "four corners of the earth" suggests a worldwide invasion, whereas Ezekiel is describing a coalition that is based primarily in the Middle East. This can be easily refuted by noting that the term "four corners of the earth" or "four winds," which are often used interchangeably,[52] are terms which often refer only to the four compass points within a Middle Eastern context (Daniel 11:4; Jeremiah 49:36).

Another reason given for dismissing Revelation 20 is that in Ezekiel, Gog is the main aggressor, a man, whereas in Revelation 20, Satan is said to be the aggressor. To this I would say that there

---

[52] See Jeremiah 49:36 and Revelation7:1.

is no reason to expect that after the Millennium Satan will be incarnate and will physically lead these nations to battle. In fact, there is explicit evidence that he operates in the same way he always has after he is released: He tempts these nations to go to war.

> Now when the thousand years have expired, Satan will be released from his prison and will go out **to deceive the nations** which are in the four corners of the earth, **Gog and Magog, to gather them together to battle**, whose number is as the sand of the sea. (Revelation 20:7–8, emphasis added)

What could be clearer than that? Satan deceives Gog and Magog to go to battle. He is not leading these armies himself. Even the simplest reading of both Ezekiel 38 and 39 and Revelation 20:7–9 proves this argument impotent, as both passages clearly say that Gog is leading human armies in each case.

Another reason given for dismissing Revelation 20:7–9 is that in the passage in Ezekiel, bones are left to be buried, but in Revelation, the fire God sends on the armies completely consumes them, bones and all. Like the others, this argument is reading way too much into the text. Let's take a look at what is said: "And fire came down from God out of heaven and devoured them" (Revelation 20:9b).

People who argue this point say the word translated "devoured" must mean the armies are completely consumed, bones and all. But I would suggest that far too little information is given here to state dogmatically that the bones must be consumed as a part of this devouring. If we look at Zechariah 14:12, which some say is a picture of the destruction of Gog and his armies, we see what looks like a fire that certainly could be described as "devouring," but apparently leaves the bones intact, as it seems to only target the soldier's flesh.

> And this shall be the plague with which the LORD will strike all the people who fought against Jerusalem: Their flesh shall dissolve while they stand on their feet, Their eyes shall dissolve in their sockets, And their tongues shall dissolve in their mouths. (Zechariah 14:12)

It's just as likely that the word John used that is translated as "devouring" can refer to an event like we find in Zechariah 14, which is limited to devouring flesh.

I hope you will see that the reasons given for dismissing Revelation 20:7–9 are easily dismissed themselves. The importance of this passage cannot be understated. If this interpretation is correct, we in fact do have a clear biblical basis for saying that the Gog-Magog war occurs after the Millennium when Satan is released.

Similarities

Despite the fact that John only spends a few verses summarizing Ezekiel's prophecy, the similarities between the two passages are striking:

1. Both armies march against Israel.
2. Both armies are destroyed by God Himself.
3. Both armies are defeated before they attack.
4. Both armies are destroyed by fire.
5. Both armies are coalitions of many countries.
6. Both armies are led by Gog.

7. The armies come upon people who have been living during an unprecedented time of peace.
8. The war will be followed by true and everlasting knowledge of God.

Problems Solved

If the Gog Magog war occurs at the end of the Millennium, as Revelation 20 says, then the following problems that the other views have are solved:

1) Yahweh's name will never be defiled again after the war is over.

2) All the passages about dwelling securely can be seen in their normal context, as Israel would have been dwelling in peace for one thousand years before this rebellion breaks out.

3) There is no need to divorce Ezekiel 38–39 from the previous chapter (chapter 37), which is part of the same prophecy and ends with a clear reference to the millennial kingdom, where Jesus is ruling over a restored Israel.

4) The millennial phrases all throughout Ezekiel can mean what they mean in other places, i.e., they are references to the Millennium.

5) References to weapons made of wood and horses can be seen literally, as opposed to being allusions to high-tech missiles, as it can be reasonably assumed that during the Millennium people will go back to a simpler way of life in which horses and wooded weapons would be used, especially if there had been no need for weapons for a thousand years.

6) The various promises of final restoration after the war, such as the cleansing of the land and a true peace with no more threats of any kind, can be seen as totally true, since there will be no more wars or evil after Satan is thrown into the lake of fire.

Arguments against a Post-Millennial Gog Magog War

1. Argument about the chronology of Ezekiel: The main reason people reject this notion is because chapters 38 and 39 in Ezekiel are followed by an obvious description of the Millennium in chapters 40–48. They assume that since chapters 40–48 talk about the Millennium, the Gog-Magog war, which is found in the two preceding chapters, must occur before the Millennium. There are indeed many occasions in Scripture where this kind of chronological connection would be valid, but, as we will see, this is definitely not one of them.

Ezekiel begins each prophecy with a description of the date when he received it; he does this thirteen times throughout the book. The section that includes the prophecy against Gog begins in chapter 33, verse 21, which says: “And it came to pass **in the twelfth year** of our captivity, in the tenth month, on the fifth day of the month, that one who had escaped from Jerusalem came to me and said, ‘The city has been captured!’” (Ezekiel 33:21, emphasis added).

Everything that Ezekiel was given to write about Gog and Magog is included in this prophecy, which continues for six chapters and ends after the section about the Gog-Magog war in chapter 39. The nine chapters that follow this prophecy about the Millennium are a part of a completely different prophecy given to Ezekiel thirteen years later! Chapter 40 begins this way: **“In the twenty-fifth year** of our captivity, at the beginning of the year, on the tenth day of the month, in the fourteenth year after the city was captured, on the very same day the hand of the LORD was upon me; and He took me there" (Ezekiel 40:1).

In his paper, "Rethinking Ezekiel's Invasion by Gog," Dr. J. Paul Tanner says, "We need not expect [chapters] 40–48 to chronologically follow [chapters] 38–39 since these chapters are part of a separate vision."

If we place the dates of Ezekiel's thirteen visions in chronological order, the list would look like this: Ezekiel 1:1; 8:1; 20:1; 24:1; 29:1; 26:1; 30:20; 31:1; 33:21; 32:1.17; 40:1; and 29:17. Notice that three of the visions are not in chronological order; more importantly, Ezekiel 29:17, which is about Egypt being conquered by Nebuchadnezzar, was written later than the prophecy of the Millennium that begins in Ezekiel 40. A simple understanding of the nature of the book of Ezekiel would prevent anyone from building doctrine based on the order of the visions in Ezekiel.

Ironically, if we apply the idea correctly and see a chronological connection within a particular vision of Ezekiel—in this case, the one that begins in chapter 33 and goes through 39—we would conclude that the Gog-Magog war must come after the Messiah is ruling on earth, since chapter 37 is so clear that the Millennium has begun and the throne of David is occupied at that time. To say it another way: if we limited chronological connections to the same vision, then it is absolutely necessary to conclude that the Gog-Magog war comes after the Millennium.

Some people even suggest that the last nine chapters of Ezekiel are a part of a separate book altogether. Josephus states that Ezekiel "left behind two books" (*The Antiquities of the Jews,* 10:5.1). And while we don't have enough information to say conclusively what Josephus meant, it would make sense if the last nine chapters of Ezekiel were distributed separately. It would mean that the book of

Ezekiel originally ended with the Gog-Magog war, which would be fitting, since the book of Revelation essentially ends with the Gog-Magog war also. Admittedly, this point is too speculative to be dogmatic about.

2. Israel would have no reason to burn the invaders' weapons or bury bodies in the eternal kingdom: There are many variations of the argument, but the main idea is based on an assumption that in the eternal state that follows the Millennium, there is no reason to bury bodies or burn weapons for fuel. The people who are making this argument assume a great deal about life after the Millennium, but the fact is that we have very little information about what life will be like in the eternal kingdom. However, the information we do have in Revelation 21–22 seems to suggest that there will indeed be life on earth, much like there was during the Millennium, and therefore there will be a reason to bury bodies and make fires.

> Then I, John, saw the holy city, New Jerusalem, coming down out of heaven from God, prepared as a bride adorned for her husband. And I heard a loud voice from heaven saying, "Behold, **the tabernacle of God is with men, and He will dwell with them**, and they shall be His people. **God Himself will be with them** and be their God. (Revelation 21:2–3, emphasis added)

The New Jerusalem is a massive structure 1,400 miles in length, width, and height. The notable point here is that this city comes from heaven to earth and "the tabernacle of God is with men, and He will dwell with them." God is going to dwell on earth in the eternal kingdom. Therefore, we would expect some semblance of the laws of nature that govern earth to be in effect during this time, even if radically modified. It should also be noted that it is prohibited for anyone to enter the New Jerusalem who might defile it.

> And they shall bring the glory and the honor of the nations into it. But there shall by no means enter it anything that defiles, or causes an abomination or a lie, but only those who are written in the Lamb's Book of Life. (Revelation 21:26–27)

I only suggest that the little information that we do have about the eternal state seems to indicate that there will be life on earth outside the New Jerusalem as well. It may be that only those who are dead in Christ dwell in this 1,400-mile-square city. But the existence of earthly life outside the city seems to be certain, and one would assume there would be need to cook food with fires, etc.

The argument that there will be no need for people to bury bodies or burn weapons in the eternal state could be a moot point anyway. After all, we are not told how much time elapses between the Gog-Magog war and the eternal state. Dr. Tanner makes the following observations regarding this:

> A closer look at Revelation 20 reveals that there are a thousand years from the beginning of Christ's millennial rule until the release of Satan. It does not tell how much time transpires between Satan's release and the eternal state. Following the thousand years, several things must take place before the eternal state: (1) Satan will be released for "a short time" (Rev. 20:3), (2) Satan will have time to deceive the nations and move them to attack Israel, (3) Satan, the beast and the false prophet will be thrown into the lake of fire (20:10), and (4) all the unrighteous

> dead will be brought before the great white throne, judged by God and thrown into the lake of fire.
>
> In all honesty, we don't know how much time there may be, but nothing in the text precludes a period of seven years in which the weapons of war could be burned. Another question, then, is: Why should an effort be made to burn the weapons if the eternal state follows shortly afterward? Perhaps, since this is the last act of war before the new creation, this is done to celebrate that Satan (the perpetrator of all wars) is forever removed and war will never again plague humanity.

So the argument concerning burning weapons and burying bodies is based on various speculations and presuppositions about things we are not yet privy to know completely, such as the timing between the thousand years and the eternal state and the exact nature of life on earth in the eternal state, but I suggest the information we do know about the eternal state certainly allows for a post-millennial Gog-Magog war.

3. Ezekiel 38–39 says that after the war "the nations shall know that I am the LORD" and that He will "make his name known" in the midst of Israel. But this would have already occurred during the Millennium.

It is true that the nations and Israel will be subservient to Christ in the Millennium, but several passages in Scripture make it known that it is far from a sin-free state (see Isaiah 65:20, 11:3–5; Zechariah 14:16–21). Those passages say that "wicked" people and "sinners" are still there. In fact, that is the probably the reason Jesus rules during this era with a "rod of iron" to quickly and decisively give out judgment to those who are sinning. It is generally accepted that during the Millennium, people will still need to accept Christ as their Savior in addition to as their King, and not everyone on earth is automatically saved.

Writer Arthur Pink said this of the millennial kingdom:

> In spite of the fact that Satan will have been removed from the earth, and that Christ reigns in person over it, yet conditions here will not be perfect even in the Millennium. Unregenerate human nature will remain unchanged. Sin will still be present, though much of its outward manifestation will be restrained. Discontent and wickedness will not be eradicated from the hearts of men, but will be kept beneath the surface by means of the Iron Rod. Multitudes will yield to Christ nothing but a "feigned obedience" (Ps. 18:44, margin). This "feigned obedience" will be the product of power not grace; it will be the fruit of fear not love.[53]

The fact that not everyone is saved is quite obvious considering that when Satan is released at the end of this thousand years, he is able to tempt so many people to go to war against Jesus that their numbers are like the "sands of the sea." The Millennium is obviously a blessed time, but it is not perfect, and it is not doctrinally correct to say that every person on earth is saved or "knows God" in the salvific sense at this time. Therefore, only after the attack described by John in Revelation 20 and the beginning of the eternal kingdom does true universal salvation appear to occur.

In conclusion, placing the Gog-Magog event at the end of the Millennium is the only option with explicit biblical support that eliminates all contradictions and invites no insurmountable

---

[53] Arthur Pink, *The Redeemer's Return*, p. 379.

criticisms. I believe the battle of Armageddon event in Revelation 16 and 19 is the second-best option, but because of the problems associated with people "dwelling securely" just before Armageddon and in light of a clear reference to the timing in Revelation 20:7, which places Gog-Magog after the Millennium, the Armageddon event should be seen as only a prefiguration or type fulfillment of the Gog-Magog war.

Chapter 12

The Gog-Magog War Part 2: Which Countries Are Involved?

Probably the most debated aspect of the Gog-Magog war concerns which countries will be involved. The desire to find out the modern equivalents of the nations mentioned by Ezekiel is particularly important for those who believe this war will occur in the near future. They argue that determining the location of these nations helps them look for the geopolitical maneuverings that indicate the war is near. As detailed in the preceding chapter, the evidence strongly supports the idea that this war will not occur until the end of the thousand-year reign of Christ on earth. This means that identifying the exact locations of the nations mentioned by Ezekiel has only limited value for the believer, since this war will be at least a thousand-plus years in the future. Attempting to force the circumstances of the war onto the modern, premillennial world can only lead to confusion and error. That being said, I do think Scripture gives us the tools we need to discover the location of many of the nations involved in this war. And I believe there is value in such a study, if for no other reason than to show the errors of the theories that try to force Ezekiel's prophecy into our modern context. I will try to remain as neutral as I can in this study, something that is uniquely possible for those who hold to the view that the Gog-Magog war won't occur until after the Millennium. If you remember from the last chapter, Christians from every era of the church have attempted to identify these countries in light of their current political circumstances; they identified the countries involved as the primary "boogey men" of their day. Because I don't need to try to fit these countries into a modern context, it is easier to follow the evidence wherever it leads. Even if you disagree with me about the timing of the war, this study on the players involved will be useful for that reason alone.

Nations Mentioned In Ezekiel 38–39

At least eleven nations are mentioned in Ezekiel 38 and 39, including Magog, Meshech, Tubal, Persia, Cush, Put, Gomer, Togarmah, Sheba, Dedan, and Tarshish. For many of these nations, there are virtually no disagreements about their location, but others have been the focus of longstanding debates. For example, few would argue that Persia refers to modern Iran, but there are many different opinions about the location of Magog, Meshech, Tubal, and others.

Millennial Occurrences

Before I start identifying the countries involved, I would like to make a point that is often overlooked by commentators, one I believe reinforces the idea that the war Ezekiel describes occurs after the Messiah has been ruling over Israel during the Millennium. Four of the countries mentioned by Ezekiel are also said to exist during the Millennium: Cush (Psalms 68:31; Isaiah 11:11; Zephaniah 3:10), Tubal (Isaiah 66:19), Sheba (Psalms 72:10; Isaiah 60:6), and Tarshish (Psalms 72:10; Isaiah 2:16, 60:9, 66:19). I could add more to this list, but will limit the references I cited to passages that unquestionably speak of the Millennium. I mention this to invoke a little humility among those attempting to identify these nations, as we simply cannot guess the exact way Christ will divide the nations during His rule. It may be that during His earthly reign, these nations will actually be called by the ancient names Ezekiel uses or have different borders. All we know for sure is that the Bible tells us that many of the nations in Ezekiel 38 and 39 are also present during the Millennium. Since we know very little about the specific division of the nations and their borders after the thousand-year rule of Christ, we must be willing to admit that precise knowledge of these nations during that time will be difficult to come by. That being said, these nations have also existed in the past, and it is possible to discover a great deal about their locations. It is reasonable to assume that the locations and borders of these countries in the past will have a great deal of correlation with their millennial counterparts.

Gog, of the Land of Magog, the Prince of Rosh, Meshech, and Tubal

Gog, the primary instigator of the war, is described as being from the land of Magog and prince over Rosh, Meshech, and Tubal: "Son of man, set your face against Gog, of the land of Magog, the prince of Rosh, Meshech, and Tubal, and prophesy against him" (Ezekiel 38:2).

Since all of the areas mentioned in this passage are a part of Gog's kingdom (Magog, Rosh, Meshech, and Tubal), determining the location of even one of these areas with a measure of certainty will help to narrow the scope of our search. I like to start any research on the location of a biblical nation within the pages of Scripture itself, because while the views of ancient writers and historians are useful, we should not rely upon them dogmatically, as they often have different opinions. While Gog, Magog, and Rosh are mentioned in other places in Scripture, those passages don't offer additional clues to their locations. Magog is only mentioned in the genealogies of Japath (Genesis 10:2; 1 Chronicles 1:5), the prophecy in Ezekiel 38–39, and in Revelation 20:8. Other than the fact that Ezekiel 38:15 says Gog will come from the "far north," we are left with no specific details that might help determine which nation or nations from the far north are being referred to. The identification of Rosh in other Scriptures is difficult as well, for reasons we will come to later. Of these four nations associated with Gog, only Meshech and Tubal are found in another place in Scripture that might give us a clue as to their whereabouts.

Meshech and Tubal

In Ezekiel 27, we find a prophecy against the city of Tyre, in modern-day Lebanon. Tyre has been a commercial shipping port for thousands of years, going back to the ancient Phoenician merchants. Ezekiel 27 describes many of the nations, including Meshech and Tubal, that traded with Tyre, as well as the specific goods they traded: "Javan, Tubal, and Meshech were your traders. They bartered human lives and vessels of bronze for your merchandise" (Ezekiel 27:13).

We can gather two important clues about Meshech and Tubal from this passage:

1. They traded with Tyre in Ezekiel's day (593–565 BC).
2. They traded bronze and slaves with Tyre.

Normally, we could gather very little about the location of a biblical nation based on the goods that it traded, but the mention of bronze narrows the field considerably. Bronze wasn't something that just anyone could make during this time; the process was very specialized and limited to a handful of nations. The field narrows even further when we consider that this nation also must be from the north and must have been able to trade with Tyre in Ezekiel's day.

This brings us to the end of the biblical clues that can help us determine the location of Meshech and Tubal. Even though it seems like only a little information, I think you will agree it is more than enough to confirm or deny the extrabiblical and historical data that we will now look at.

The *Jewish Encyclopedia* identifies the Meshech and Tubal with Moschia (which the Assyrians called "Mushki" or "Muski") and Tubal (which the Assyrians called "Tabal").

> The Meshech...are probably the Moschi (Assyrian: Mushku and Musku), the inhabitants of the Moschian mountains, between the Black and the Caspian seas, which contained rich copper mines. "Tubal" (Assyrian, Tabal), which is always mentioned in connection with Meshech, is the name of the Tibareni, who lived to the south-east of the Black sea.[54]

There are many reasons to take this view seriously. I mentioned before that the production of bronze was important. Well, Mushku and Tabal were one of the few places in the world where bronze was produced at this time; in fact, they were famous for it—they were even one of the inventors of Iron Age metallurgy. The legend of King Midas, who was said to be able to turn everything he touched into gold, is actually based on Mita, a historic king of Moschia. Assyrian records refer to the Assyrians receiving huge amounts of bronze vessels as tribute from Moschia and Tabal—the very goods that Ezekiel said these nations traded with. In addition, it is known that trade between these countries and Tyre was well established at the time of Ezekiel's writing.

---

[54] "Armenia." *Jewish Encyclopedia*, 1906. http://www.jewishencyclopedia.com/articles/1787-armenia.

It is interesting that these two places, Moschia and Tabal, are so often mentioned together in ancient writings, because Meshech and Tubal are also almost always mentioned together in the Bible, too (Ezekiel 27:13, 32:26, 38:2, 3, 39:1; Genesis 10:2). One scholar believes that even Rosh is mentioned along with Meshech and Tubal in one Assyrian text.

> There is even one cuneiform document from the reign of the Assyrian King Sargon II (ruled 722–705 B.C.) which actually names all three peoples [Rosh, Meshech, Tubal] mentioned by Ezekiel 38–39. Sargon II writes in this badly broken inscription:
>
> I deported (the people) of the lands of Kashu, **Tabalu**, and Hilakku. I drove out Mite (Midas), king of the land of **Muski**...the lands of **Rashi** and Ellipi which are on the Elamite frontier.[55] (emphasis added)

This view is also consistent with what we know from ancient writers like Josephus, who identified the people from Meshech and Tubal as the Mosocheni (from Moschia) and Thobelites (from Tabal). The identification of Meshech and Tubal as Moschia and Tabal has a massive amount of support in the modern scholarly community as well.[56] It's probably safe to call it the majority view among scholars.

---

[55] Clyde Billington. "The Rosh People in History and Prophecy," vol. 3: *Michigan Theological Journal* Volume 3. 1992 (2) (170–171). Plymouth, Michigan: Michigan Theological Seminary.

[56] R. H. Alexander, "A Fresh Look at Ezekiel 38 and 39, " in JETS 17 (1974), pp. 161 f.; E. M. Blaiklock, *Pictorial Bible Atlas* (Grand Rapids: Zondervan, 1969), p. 45; John J. Davis, *Paradise to Prison* (Grand Rapids: Baker, 1975), pp. 138 f.; J. D. Douglas, ed., *The New Bible Dictionary* (Grand Rapids: Eerdmans, 1962), p. 811; C. F. Pfeiffer, H. F. Vos, and J. Rea, eds., *Wycliffe Bible Encyclopedia* (Chicago: Moody,

A few people have claimed that Meshech and Tubal refer to the modern Russian cities of Moscow and Tobolsk. There is no historical support for this claim whatsoever. It is based solely on the similar sounds of both words. Even people like Thomas Ice who support the idea that Russia is in view with the northern coalition of Gog reject the idea that Meshech and Tubal indicate Moscow and Tobolsk.[57]

The modern location of Meshech and Tubal is on the southeast side of the Black Sea, south of the Caucuses Mountains, primarily in modern-day Georgia as well as parts of Armenia and eastern Turkey. There is some debate as to whether Tubal should also be associated with the Tibareni on the Black Sea coast, which would push the location a bit more into central Turkey, but that connection is not as certain.

Gog and Magog

The location of Gog and Magog are much more difficult to determine, either with Scripture or historical accounts. Gog, of course, is a proper name designating the leader of this future coalition. Some people attempt to find a reference to a king named Gog in ancient texts, namely Gugu of Lydia (western Turkey), but the general consensus seems to be that this connection is inconclusive.

The location of Magog is also less clear than Tubal or Meshech. There is not very much to go on in Scripture or history, though we can reasonably assume that Magog would be close to Meshech and

---

1975), II, pp. 1105 f., 1751;J. B. Taylor, Ezekiel (London: Tyndale, 1969), p. 244.

[57] Thomas D. Ice, "Ezekiel 38 & 39" (2009). Article Archives. Paper 1, http://digitalcommons.liberty.edu/pretrib_arch/1 .

Tubal based on the biblical account that seems to link the three nations, and the fact that the migrations of Japheth's sons would likely be close together. Jewish sources have traditionally put Magog very close to Meshech and Tubal (see map).

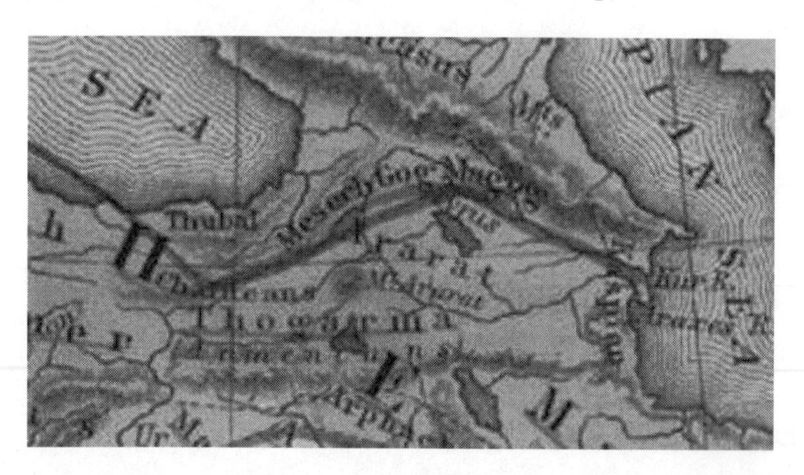

Josephus said: "Magog founded those that from him were named Magogites, but who are by the Greeks called Scythians."[58] The Scythians were a band of ethnically diverse nomadic tribes that spanned great distances in the Eurasian Steppe. There are several problems with understanding the term "Scythians" used by Josephus the same way we do today. The term was applied very generally by the Greeks as any nomadic tribe north of the Black Sea. Other scholars have pointed out that the terms "Scythians" and "Cimmerians" were used interchangeably.[59] The Cimmerians started out dwelling north of the Caucuses Mountains, but by Ezekiel's day had migrated south due to wars with Sargon II, settling in the general area of Meshech and Tubal, specifically around modern-day Armenia, Georgia, and parts of Turkey. The *Encyclopedia Biblica* places Magog in the same area using a

---

58 Flavius Josephus, *Antiquities of the Jews*, Book 6, chapter 1.

59 Maurits Nanning Van Loon. *Urartian Art. Its Distinctive Traits in the Light of New Excavations*, Istanbul, 1966, p. 16.

totally different method to come to its conclusion.[60] I believe that the evidence is conclusive that Magog should be placed in roughly the same area as Meshech and Tubal, in modern-day Georgia, Armenia, and eastern Turkey.

The Rosh Problem

There is considerable debate among scholars to this day as to whether the Hebrew word "Rosh" in Ezekiel 38:3 is a proper noun designating another nation or an adjective related to "prince" (i.e., "chief prince"). A review of different Bible translations will demonstrate the differences in opinion among scholars:

- …and say, "Thus says the Lord GOD: 'Behold, I am against you, O Gog, **the prince of Rosh**, Meshech, and Tubal.'" (Ezekiel 38:3, NKJV, emphasis added)

- …and say, Thus says the Lord GOD: Behold, I am against you, O Gog, **chief prince of Meshech** and Tubal. (Ezekiel 38:3, ESV, emphasis added)

The basic idea is that if "Rosh" is a proper noun, then Gog is also the prince of a place named Rosh. If it's not a proper noun, then it should be translated as the word "chief," meaning that Gog is the chief prince of only Meshech and Tubal, and there is no place called Rosh. This argument seems to be primarily motivated by those trying to either prove a connection to Rosh and modern-day Russia and those who are trying to deny such a connection. In my opinion, both sides are letting their determination to prove their points affect their ability to honestly deal with the issue.

---

[60] *Encyclopedia Biblica,* 1899. Entry on "Gog and Magog."

The early Greek texts of the Old Testament such as the Septuagint and the Theodosian translate "Rosh" as a proper noun. But Jerome, when writing his Latin translation of the Bible known as the Vulgate, decided to translate "Rosh" as "chief." He did this not because of any grammatical clue, but rather, in his own words, because "we could not find the name of this race [i.e., the Rosh people] mentioned either in Genesis or any other place in the Scriptures, or in Josephus."[61]

Though Jerome couldn't find any references to the Rosh people, there do indeed seem to be such references in ancient history. Clyde E. Billington, in his three-part paper, "The Rosh People in History and Prophecy," does a good job of tracking down the references to the Rosh people. I disagree with part 3 of Billington's paper, in which he claims that the references to "Rosh" in Ezekiel should be understood as modern-day Russia, but I do agree with him that the Rosh were an ancient people in Ezekiel's day.

The Rosh people, according to Billington, migrated often during their history, but he believes that they primarily occupied a particular area south of the Caucasus Mountains in modern Armenia, Azerbaijan, Georgia, and northeastern Turkey.[62] In other words, he agrees that the Rosh were located in the same areas as Meshech, Tubal, and Magog. It is especially notable that this was the primary location of the Rosh people when, as mentioned earlier, the Rosh were mentioned in the same Assyrian inscription with Meshech and Tubal, which links them all to the same basic geographic region.

---

[61] Jerome, *Commentariorum in Ezechielem*, col. 357.
[62] Billington, 168.

Billington and others who attempt to equate the Rosh mentioned by Ezekiel to modern Russia do so by arguing that the Rosh people, long after the time of Ezekiel, migrated north of the Caucuses to modern-day Ukraine. They also argue that the Varangian Rus, Vikings of Scandinavian origin who conquered Russia from the north in the ninth century AD and are why we call the land Russia today, got the second part of their name (Rus) from intermarriage with the Rosh people in the south in an attempt to integrate with their conquered population. While this argument is feasible, from what I can tell, I also believe that this has little bearing on the identification of the Rosh in Ezekiel 38 and 39 for the following reasons:

1. It is clear that Ezekiel believed that Magog, Rosh, Meshech, and Tubal were closely related. And given the fact that in Ezekiel's day, even Billington admits, all of these places were geographically centered in the areas around Georgia, Armenia, and eastern Turkey, it is far more reasonable to assume that this is the area the northern coalition will come from.

2. Ezekiel 27 not only mentions Meshech and Tubal as trading with Tyre, but also almost every other nation that is a part of this future war, namely Put, Togarmah, Dedan, Sheba, Tarshish, and Persia. It is inconceivable to think that Russia was trading with Tyre in Ezekiel's day.

3. The method of interpretation that Billington and others use is called the ancestral migration method, which attempts to identify nations in Scripture not by the geographic location of the nation during the relevant times, but rather by tracing the bloodlines of the people throughout history. Joel Richardson, in his book *Mideast Beast,* makes the following statement about this method of interpretation: "The ancestral-migration method is fraught with difficulties, dangers, and inconsistencies and should be avoided

altogether by all who seek to responsibly interpret biblical prophecy."

The bottom line is that all the nations mentioned in Ezekiel 38:3—Magog, Rosh, Meshech, and Tubal, as well as the other nations we are about to look at that are involved in the northern coalition of the Gog Magog war—can all be shown to have been located in modern-day Georgia, Armenia, and Turkey, a relatively small area to the far north of Israel, that traded with Tyre with the same goods mentioned in Ezekiel 27. There is every reason to believe that this will be the area the northern coalition will come from in the future war as well. Anyone who says differently is trying to force his or her presuppositions on the text, in my opinion.

Persia

Ezekiel 38: 5 continues listing nations that will play a role in the Gog-Magog war when it says "Persia, Cush, and Put are with them, all of them with shield and helmet." There is far less dispute about the location of these nations among scholars and commentators. As mentioned earlier, there is virtually no disagreement that Persia is equated with modern Iran. In fact it was only in 1959 that Iran changed its name from Persia to Iran, and there is no reason to see Ezekiel referring to any other nation.

Cush

Cush, often translated "Ethiopia," is considered by most scholars to be the area directly south of Egypt, including parts of modern Sudan, Ethiopia, Eritrea, and Somalia, especially along the Nile River and the lands near the Red Sea.

Put

Put or Phut is often translated as "Libya," and refers to most of northwestern Africa west of Egypt, including modern Libya, Algeria, Tunisia, and Morocco.

Gomer

Though there was a theory in the early 1900s that Gomer referred to Germany, the idea has been rejected in more modern times because of etymological factors.[63] Today, virtually all Bible scholars[64] believe that Gomer refers to the Cimmerians,[65] who were referred to as "Gimirru" in Akkadian, and were dwelling in the same area as many of the northern nations mentioned earlier: Georgia, Armenia, and Turkey.

Togarmah

Togarmah is identified with the Anatolian kingdom called Tegarama by the Hittites and Til-Garimmu by the Assyrians. It was very near to Tubal and Meshach in modern-day Georgia and Armenia and parts of Turkey.

---

63 Stuart Piggot (1968). *The Druids,* Thames and Hudson: London, pp. 132, 172.

64 *Holman Bible Atlas, Oxford Bible Atlas, The IVP Atlas of Bible History, New Bible Atlas, The Macmillan Bible Atlas, Zondervan Atlas of the Bible, Zondervan Illustrated Bible Backgrounds Commentary, New Moody Atlas of the Bible, Baker Bible Atlas.*

65 *Cambridge Ancient History* Vol. II, pt. 2, p. 425.

A Need for Clarity

Too many commentators these days are not giving people all the information they need when discussing the locations of these countries. For example, those who are trying to make all of these countries Muslim tend to make general statements that the northern nations are simply in Turkey (a mostly secular nation, but admittedly one with Islamic leanings), as opposed to being clear that the northern nations mentioned by Ezekiel are often primarily in Georgia and Armenia—an idea that those holding to the Islamic view don't like, since both of those countries are decidedly Christian today. Conversely, those wanting to push the Russian view often try to make general statements about these nations being near modern-day Russia without going into exact details of their locations, which tend to diminish that connection. Or, as we saw earlier, they will admit that the nations were not in Russia in Ezekiel's day, but say that a few of them did migrate to Russia 1,700 years later.

A Possible Reason the Countries Surrounding Israel Are Not Mentioned

If you look at all of the areas that will be involved in the Gog-Magog war (see map) an interesting question comes up: Why aren't the nations closest to Israel involved? It seems there is a kind of buffer zone of nations that separate Israel from its enemies.

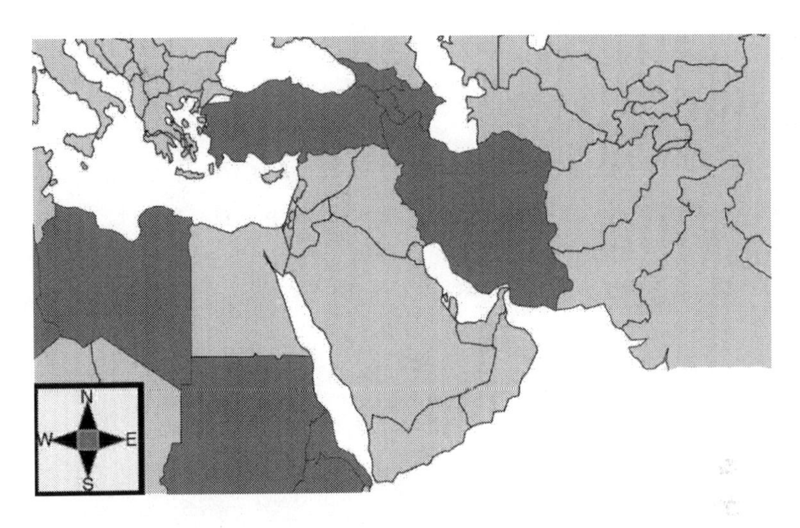

Why, for example, isn't Egypt involved? Historically, it has been a major enemy of Israel, not to mention of Jordan, Saudi Arabia, Iraq, and Syria, which constitute the biblical Assyria. The answer lies in Isaiah 19:23–25, which says that during the Millennium, Egypt and Assyria will be in a special relationship with the Lord and Israel.

> In that day there will be a highway from Egypt to Assyria, and the Assyrian will come into Egypt and the Egyptian into Assyria, and the Egyptians will serve with the Assyrians. In that day Israel will be one of three with Egypt and Assyria—a blessing in the midst of the land, whom the LORD of hosts shall bless, saying, "Blessed is Egypt My people, and Assyria the work of My hands, and Israel My inheritance." (Isaiah 19:23–25)

So it would seem that those closest to Israel, namely Egypt and Assyria, will be allied with Israel in a special way during the Millennium, and when the time comes for Satan to be released at the end of the thousand-year period, they remain true to the Lord. I believe this is the best way to explain the conspicuous absence of these historical enemies of Israel in the Gog-Magog war.

In this chapter, I have discussed the fact that many of the nations involved in the Gog-Magog war are also explicitly said to be in the Millennium. I have gone over the biblical and historical evidence for the locations of the primary players in the war and shown that most of the disputed nations were south of the Caucuses Mountains in the areas occupied by Georgia, Armenia, Turkey, Iran, Egypt, and Libya. Finally, I have tried to explain the conspicuous absence of Egypt, Jordan, Saudi Arabia, Iraq, and Syria from the Gog-Magog war by citing the prophet Isaiah, who said that those nations will be in a special relationship with the Lord during the Millennium and therefore will be unlikely to rebel against Him when Satan is released.

Chapter 13

Problems with the Psalm 83 War

In the next chapter, I will explain why getting the Gog-Magog war timing wrong could play into the hands of the Antichrist. But before I do that, I need to discuss the so-called Psalm 83 war, because believing that this war will take place is just as dangerous as believing false views about the Gog-Magog war for many of the same reasons.

Psalm 83 is a prayer of Asaph that describes many of Israel's closest neighbors plotting against it. Asaph is praying for God to destroy the nations that are scheming against Israel. In times past, this psalm has been seen simply as a prayer of Asaph that asks God to help Israel by dealing with its many enemies during Asaph's day. However, recently, a new doctrine has come about, chiefly through Arnold Fruchtenbaum and Bill Salus, that suggests that the prayer of Asaph in Psalm 83 should be seen as a prophecy, because, they say, such a war has never occurred in Israel's history and therefore must be seen as a future event.

I will be arguing against this theory by making the following points:

1. There is no war in Psalm 83.
2. There is no prophecy in Psalm 83.
3. All the events in Psalm 83 happened in Asaph's day.
4. Similar prayers in other psalms obviously are not prophecies.

5. Bill Salus' responses when challenged on this theory are not convincing.

There Is No War in Psalm 83

A plain reading of Psalm 83 suggests nothing more than that a number of nations in Asaph's day had recently been making political alliances against Israel; they never actually attacked anyone. The phrases used to describe their actions include: "They have taken crafty counsel," "They have said," "For they have consulted together," and, "They form a confederacy." The phrases describing what these nations are doing show them simply making alliances and plans; nothing in the text describes these nations doing anything more than that. The whole point of Asaph's prayer is to ask God to prevent these nations from doing anything more than simply planning to attack. And if God answered Asaph's prayer, then there is no reason to go looking for this war in history or the future, because God prevented it from happening as per Asaph's request. I challenge anyone to show evidence of a war in Psalm 83—it cannot be done.

There Is No Prophecy in Psalm 83

No language in Psalm 83 suggests that it is prophetic. In other prophecies of future wars or judgments upon nations, the prophet often declares that he is speaking a prophecy by saying something like, "The Lord said that in the latter years such and such will happen," as in the case of Ezekiel 38:8, or, "At the time of the end, so and so will attack," as in Daniel 11:40. In addition, prophecies in the Psalms often describe events in the Messianic Age to signify that a prophecy is being made, or there is some sort of response from God, or some clear reference to Jesus in the psalm. These are certainly not the only ways we can tell if a passage is prophetic, but they are by far the most common. Psalm 83 has none of these elements, and as we will see the reasons that Bill Salus says Psalm 83 is prophetic are not at all convincing. Asaph never says he is seeing something that will take place in the future; in fact, every indication from the text we have suggests that he is describing the political situation of his own day.

All the Events in Psalm 83 Happened in Asaph's Day

The political situation that Asaph describes in Psalm 83 is perfectly consistent with events in his day (around 950 BC), and there is no reason to see this psalm as requiring future fulfillment. The nations he mentions conspiring together, such as Edom, Moab, Hagrites, Gebal, Ammon, Amalek, Philistia, Tyre, Assyria, and Lot, were all very close neighbors to Israel (mostly in Jordan and Lebanon). The picture painted by Asaph is a perfect fit with what we know from Scripture and history about the political situation of the time. Bill Salus would disagree with this point, and I will deal with his arguments in the final section of this chapter.

Similar Prayers in Other Psalms Obviously Are Not Prophecies

On several occasions in the Psalms, we see the psalmist complaining to God about the surrounding nations that wanted to see Israel destroyed. The psalmists often plead with God to destroy these enemies. Anyone who has spent much time reading the Psalms will know that this is a consistent if not prevalent theme throughout the book. Therefore, without any direct reason to do otherwise in the text, we should assume that Psalm 83 is like all the other prayers for deliverance from enemies of the day that were not prophetic.

Bill Salus' Responses When Challenged on This Theory

In a recent debate with Thomas Ice, Bill Salus was challenged with many of the points I have brought up in this chapter. I will list his responses to Ice's criticisms, with my comments. In response to Ice's suggestion that there is no prophecy in Psalm 83, Salus made the following points:

1. Salus said that Asaph was called a "seer" in 2 Chronicles 29:30 and so should be considered a prophet.

This is true. But establishing Asaph as a prophet has nothing to do with whether Psalm 83 is a prophecy. David was a prophet, but very few aspects of his psalms are considered prophecies. Daniel was a prophet, but plenty of his writings are not prophetic (his account of being thrown into the lion's den, etc.). Just because a prophet is a prophet does not mean that every word he wrote was prophetic.

2. Salus claims that Assyria and Gebal, both mentioned in Psalm 83, were not "in the picture" or "in the fray" during the time of Asaph, therefore, Psalm 83 must be a prophecy.

Assyria

By Asaph's day, Assyria had been in existence for more than one thousand years. Even the Middle Kingdom of Assyria, the kingdom in question, was established nearly four hundred years prior to Asaph. In addition we know of Assyria/Israel relations at least as far back as 871–850 BC because of Assyrian inscriptions that mention King Ahab and Jehu of Israel, which would have been only seventy-five to one hundred years after Asaph wrote.

Considering what Assyria was doing as a part of the coalition in Psalm 83—namely, helping the Ammonites and Moabites, which probably means supplying soldiers or other types of aid to them—we can be more certain that this fits with what we know of the political situation of the day. During the reign of David, who wrote many of the psalms, the Ammonites had procured soldiers from Syria to defend itself against King David, according to 2 Samuel 10:6:

> When the people of Ammon saw that they had made themselves repulsive to David, the people of Ammon sent and hired the Syrians of Beth Rehob and the Syrians of Zoba, twenty thousand foot soldiers; and from the king of Maacah one thousand men, and from Ish-Tob twelve thousand men. (2 Samuel 10:6)

This is very significant because it shows that what Psalm 83 said Ammon and Moab were doing—getting help from countries to the north to fight Israel—was something they had done only a few years before Asaph wrote.

The motive for Assyria to help Ammon and Moab is obvious, because in 950 BC, trade routes such as the King's Highway, which was always a source of wars between Trans-Jordan and Israel (see Numbers 20:17–21), was more important than ever. The recent expansion of Israel during the reign of David and Solomon had severely threatened access to these routes, which were a lifeline to the Assyrian Empire. If Ammon and Moab, along with their allies, could conquer even a small amount of land to secure these routes, the financial benefits to Assyria would be vast. Ammon and Moab had a unique relationship with Assyria. In the late eighth century, they were allies with Assyria, paying it regular tribute, as opposed to being conquered by Assyria, as many of its neighbors.[66]

Bill Salus says that Psalm 83 has to be a prophecy, because Assyria was not "in the picture" at the time; yet, everything we know from archeological finds suggests that it was very much in the picture.

Gebal

Salus says that Gebal wasn't "in the fray" during Asaph's day, but this is untrue. Gebal, or modern-day Byblos, in Lebanon is considered the oldest continually inhabited city in the world, with a history going back thousands of years before Asaph. Gebal is even mentioned in 1 Kings 5:18,[67] which would put it having relations with Israel during the time in question. In addition, we know that Assyrian King Tiglath-Pileser I (1114–1076 BC) visited Gebal to secure trade routes there,[68] which might explain why Lebanon and Jordan were banding together with Assyrian support in Psalm 83: to secure trade routes to Assyria that flowed from Lebanon to the King's Highway, which were being hampered by Israel's expansion.

3. Salus says the phrase "tents of Edom" must refer to the modern-day Palestinians.

---

[66] "The Old Testament Kingdoms of Jordan." Archived from the original on 6 May 2009. Retrieved 2009-05-12.

[67] In 1 Kings 5:18, the word often translated "stonesquarers" (H1382 giblîy) means "inhabitants of Gebal."

[68] David Kertai, *The History of the Middle Assyrian Empire,* Atlanta, XL–XLI (2008–2009), pp. 41–42.

Salus says the word "tents" in Psalm 83:6 suggests a "habitation condition," and, since, in his view, the people of Edom "have ethnical representation in the Palestinians today," this phrase must be seen as a prophecy.

Salus is trying to use the reference to "tents" as a technical term that applies to the current Palestinian refugee conditions, but this is absurd, and ignores the reason the phrase "tents of Edom" was used. The Edomites were semi-nomadic, pastoral people who really did dwell in tents. One archeologist notes that "Moab, and especially Edom, should be considered mainly as 'tented kingdoms,' likewise, in at any rate the 13th to perhaps the 9th centuries BC, as a result."[69]

Since the people of Edom dwelled in tents, Asaph refers to them as "the tents of Edom" It's as simple as that.

In addition, Edom was located south of the Red Sea, mostly in modern-day Jordan. It was directly below the kingdom of Moab in the east and below the kingdom of Judah in the west. Today, there are no Palestinian territories in what was ancient Edom. Salus is saying that the Palestinians today have Edomite blood, even though they don't dwell in Edom anymore. I can't imagine how one could prove that claim unless a comprehensive study of the migration of the Palestinians was done alongside a massive genetic testing campaign. Even if we assumed Salus' assertion was true, notice how inconsistent his hermeneutic is. In all other cases in Psalm 83, Salus is looking at the geographic areas mentioned and matching them with their modern equivalents. For example, when the psalm mentions Gebal in Lebanon, Salus is looking to that area in Lebanon and trying to match it with people living in that

---

[69] *Early Edom and Moab, Egyptian Evidence on Ancient Jordan*; K. A. Kitchen, ed.: Piotr Bienkowski, 1992.

location. In that case, it doesn't seem to matter to him who carries modern Gebal blood. But, in the case of Edom, he doesn't seem to care who dwells in the land of Edom; he is only interested in the bloodline of the people who lived there in Asaph's day. One can argue which method of interpretation is correct, but we can't have it both ways without major inconsistencies and contradictions.

The point is that Salus takes something very simple, the phrase "tents of Edom," a reference to the tent-dwelling people of Edom, and says that it can only refer to modern-day Palestinians refugees, even though they don't dwell in Edom!

Conclusion

The Psalm 83 war is a brand-new doctrine, which, to quote Thomas Ice, is "utter speculation." In Psalm 83, Asaph is praying for God to deal with various enemies around Israel who are making political alliances that might one day lead them to attack Israel. There are no descriptions of a war or an attack of any kind in Psalm 83, nor is there any language that suggests Asaph is making a prophecy. Asaph's prayer is almost identical to other prayers in the Psalms where the writer asks God to stop various enemies who are plotting against Israel. From everything we can tell in Scripture and in history, the political alliances being made are consistent with Asaph's time. I dealt with Bill Salus' responses to Thomas Ice's critiques of his theory and showed that both Assyria and Gebal were "in the fray" during the time in question, as well as showed that the phrase "tents of Edom" simply refers to those who dwell in Edom.

Chapter 14

Faking the Gog Magog War and Armageddon

In this chapter, I will attempt to show how the Antichrist could use popular but wrong beliefs about the Gog-Magog war and the battle of Armageddon to make it seem as if he is the Jewish Messiah or even Jesus Himself. I already talked about many aspects of this deception in chapter 7, "The Disastrous Results of Jewish and Islamic Eschatology," and that chapter should be considered preliminary reading to this one. In this chapter I want to focus on Christian views of Armageddon and the Gog-Magog war, and how they could be exploited by the Antichrist.

To Christians—indeed, to many people in the secular world—there can be no return of the Messiah without a battle of Armageddon. This is one of those non-negotiable aspects of eschatology that spans almost all belief systems. If the Antichrist is going to try to deceive people in this way, he is going to have to fake the battle of Armageddon and win it in order to validate his Messianic claims.

I am not sure whether the Antichrist will attempt to fake two separate wars (Gog-Magog and Armageddon) or if he will make it seem like the wars he fights described in Daniel 11:40–45 are the fulfillment of both of these wars. Since there are so many similarities between the Gog-Magog war and the battle of Armageddon, and since most Christians and Jews already see the two wars as being one and the same, I lean toward the view that he will make no distinction between them. I suggest that he will lead people to believe that when he defends himself and Israel from virtually the entire Middle East in a miraculous way, it should be seen as the fulfillment of all known eschatological wars, and that the Messianic Age has come.

Why Are Incorrect Views about These Wars Dangerous?

The belief that the Gog-Magog war will occur before the Millennium, a view I argued against in a previous chapter, is dangerous for a few reasons. First, it makes people believe that a war with the Muslim world is a necessary part of the end-time scenario. This is because, unlike the references to the battle of Armageddon, where no specific nations are mentioned, the Ezekiel passages about the Gog-Magog war name certain nations like Persia in Iran and Turkey that are mostly Muslim nations today. It doesn't matter whether someone believes that Gog-Magog and Armageddon are the same event or are separated by a few years, the effect is still the same: It makes people believe a war with Islam is in the near future. The same is true with the belief in a Psalm 83 war. The belief that we are all to be expecting a war with the Muslims and that the Messiah will emerge victorious from that war will be exploited by the Antichrist, for reasons I will soon discuss.

As detailed previously, I also believe that the Gog-Magog war will occur. But when it does take place, at the end of the thousand-year reign (Revelation 20:7–8), it won't be with people who believe in the Islamic faith. It is impossible to know the mindset of the people who attack Israel after the Millennium, but one thing is certain: Islam will not be a viable religion during the thousand-year reign of Christ. And it's unlikely that it will be revived when Satan is released from the pit after the thousand years, either, given the fact that all the major tenets of Islam will have been unquestionably refuted one thousand years prior to the event. In addition, Islam will not play a role in the battle of Armageddon due to the fact that the people who fight in that war will be firm adherents to the religion of the Antichrist, which requires them to worship a man who had recently fought a war with the Islamic world and is sitting in the Jewish temple as God! These things simply cannot be reconciled with Islam in any form. To say that the war of Armageddon is with those believing in Islam as opposed to the religion of Antichrist is absurd for those reasons. In other words, neither the battle of Armageddon nor the Gog-Magog war will havc anything to do with Islam. Yct, this has bccomc a prevailing belief among prophecy teachers. What is the problem with that thinking? And how could it be exploited by the Antichrist?

As discussed in chapter 7, the Antichrist will easily be able to manipulate the Muslim world into attacking him by claiming to be the Messiah, whom it will see as the Dajjal. His rebuilding the temple and starting the daily sacrifices will also incite the Muslim world to attack him, as seen in Daniel 11:40–45. If Christians can be convinced that the Muslims are the enemy that needs to be defeated in order to usher in the Messianic Age, then they will reflexively see the wars that the Antichrist fights against the Muslims as the Gog-Magog war, the war of Armageddon, or both. The obvious problem with this is that since the Antichrist wins the wars in Daniel 11, and Scripture says God wins the wars of Gog-Magog and Armageddon, the Antichrist will be seen as God by Christians and Jews when he emerges victorious from the wars of Daniel 11:40–45. Essentially, the Antichrist will be creating an artificial Gog-Magog/Armageddon war way before any of these wars actually take place in order to convince people that the reign of the Messiah has come.

The following chart shows the chronology of these events.

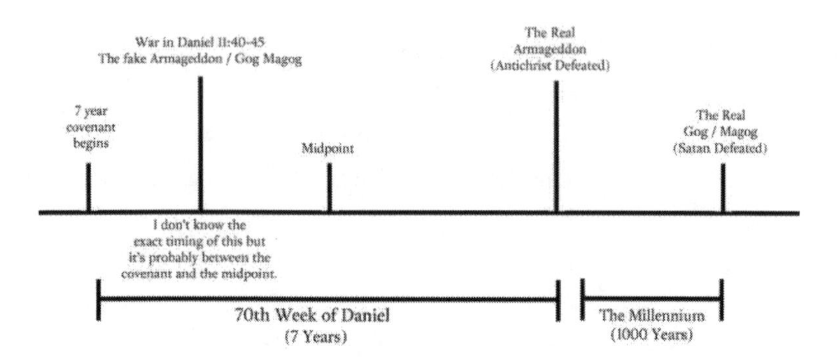

It should be said that the illustration depicts my best guess. By their very nature, the deceptions of the Antichrist are difficult to anticipate, and I am not dogmatic that it must play out exactly as I suggest. I am only putting forth one possible theory that I think best explains the evidence. Regardless of the details, however, the fact that that the Antichrist is attacked by the Muslim world and then defeats it before making his claim to be God and starting a fake Messianic Age should suggest that he will attempt to look like the savior of Israel. Many modern prophecy teachers are telling their students that when they see an attack by the Muslim world and then see it defeated, they will know that the person who does that is God. This should be seen as the terrible danger that it is. We are being set up to see the Antichrist as God. I have to say that, from the state of modern prophecy teaching, the Antichrist stands a pretty good chance of convincing more of us than we would have ever thought possible.

Appendix A

The Revived Roman Empire Revisited

We find Nebuchadnezzar's dream of the statue in Daniel 2. I will attempt to establish that while the last empire being spoken of there is indeed Rome, the Babylonian king's vision was not intended to give us information about the end times like Daniel's vision in chapter 7 is. Nebuchadnezzar's vision was intended to be a prophecy of the first coming of Jesus Christ and the establishment of the kingdom of God that would one day grow to encompass all the earth—a kingdom that Jesus said was established during the days of his earthly ministry; i.e., during the Roman Empire (Matthew 12:28, 13:31–33 Luke 17:20–21, Mark 1:15).

Let's first study the last part of Daniel 2 in order to show that this view that Nebuchadnezzar's dream is a self-contained unit not intended to be seen as a prophecy of the end times has strong biblical support.

Nebuchadnezzar's Vision of a Statue

> **Daniel 2:40** And the fourth kingdom shall be as strong as iron, inasmuch as iron breaks in pieces and shatters everything; and like iron that crushes, that kingdom will break in pieces and crush all the others.
> **Daniel 2:41** Whereas you saw the feet and toes, partly of potter's clay and partly of iron, the kingdom shall be divided; yet the strength of the iron shall be in it, just as you saw the iron mixed with ceramic clay.

Daniel 2:42 And as the toes of the feet were partly of iron and partly of clay, so the kingdom shall be partly strong and partly fragile.
Daniel 2:43 As you saw iron mixed with ceramic clay, they will mingle with the seed of men; but they will not adhere to one another, just as iron does not mix with clay.

Daniel 2:44 And in the days of these kings the God of heaven will set up a kingdom which shall never be destroyed; and the kingdom shall not be left to other people; it shall break in pieces and consume all these kingdoms, and it shall stand forever.

I agree that these feet and toes are somehow a part of the Roman Empire. In other words, the feet and toes mixed with iron and clay, while different, are not a part of a new kingdom, but are a part of the legs of iron, which indicates the Roman Empire—just a chronologically later part of it, i.e., the end. Most conservative scholars tend to agree with this interpretation, but with some of the following variations:

1. The feet and toes represent the final period of the Roman Empire being divided, weak, and trying to cleave its divided empire together but failing.

2. The feet and toes represent the final kingdom of the Antichrist in the last days.

3. The feet and toes represent a nephilim[70] hybrid kingdom in the last days.

---

[70] The nephilim were offspring of the "sons of God" and the "daughters of men" before the Deluge according to Genesis 6:4; the name is also used

I agree with conservative scholar Stephen Miller that in addition to your view of Daniel 2 and 7, your view about the rock that destroys this statue is the key to interpreting this passage. I ask you to withhold your judgment on this matter until we get to those verses.

The Kingdom Shall Be Divided

A very important part of this discussion is that the last kingdom at some point will be divided. Since most views rightly presume that the feet and toes represent a chronologically later point of Rome, we can safely say that this indicates that Rome will be divided toward the end of its existence, whether we believe that its end *was* in thc past or *will be* in the future.

Here we have a few problems for the revived Roman Empire view. The first is that we have an unambiguous fulfillment of this passage in the history of the fall of Rome. We know that Rome was divided into several parts before its fall, eventually settling into just two parts: the east and west empires. The second major problem here for the revived Roman Empire view is that forcing this prophecy to the end times means that we have to hold the view that the Antichrist has a divided, weak kingdom in the end times.

The descriptions of the Antichrist's kingdom in the Bible do not give the impression that it will be weak or divided, but rather that he will have absolute power, and that those who do not worship him will be killed. This does not sound like a weak or divided kingdom.

---

in reference to giants who inhabited Canaan at the time of the Israelite conquest of Canaan according to Numbers 13:33.

If we look up the phrase, "the crisis of the third century," we learn about a one hundred-year-or-so period in Roman history when the empire almost lost everything. It was the first time in Rome's history that it started to show weakness. All the years of Roman dominance and iron-fisted—or should I say "iron-legged"—rule was starting to slow down during this time.

In AD 285, Diocletian split the empire into four parts called the tetrarchy, but it didn't last. It briefly was united again under Constantine, but after his death it quickly split again into three divisions. It was total chaos, everyone claiming to be emperor for a few years.

Eventually, when all the dust settled, there were only two divisions of Rome: the eastern half and western half. That is how it would stay until Rome fizzled out of existence. Rome would never again rise to the prominence it once had, and it will grow less and less powerful until it is a shadow of its former self, constantly sacked by invading barbarians, penniless, and powerless. The exact date of Rome's fall varies because of the death-by-a-thousand-cuts nature of its decline, but most historians put its fall at about AD 480, a mere one hundred years after the division of east and west was solidified.

I'm trying to establish that the end of Rome is characterized by weakness and division, and, as noted before, the one thing both sides of the argument about the feet and toes made of iron and clay agree on is that this passage is saying that the end of the Roman Empire will be characterized by weakness and division. The only difference is that some say the end of the Roman Empire is in the past, and others say we need to "revive" a Roman Empire first, and *then* watch its end be characterized by weakness and division.

The Kingdom Shall Be Partly Strong and Partly Fragile

Again, this is a terrific description of the last three hundred or so years of the Roman Empire. There were times during this period, often called "the decline of the Roman Empire," in which Rome was **partly strong** in some ways, but **partly fragile** in others.

We have seen already to an extent, and will see again in the next verse, that it is grammatically necessary to see that the clay and iron represent the *two divisions* of the empire, in this case, the east and the west empires. So, in order for this interpretation to be a perfect match, we need to see a clear description in history of one of these divisions being much weaker than the other.

The so-called "final split" of the Roman Empire occurred when it was becoming clear that the Western Empire was going to be a lot more dangerous place to live than the east. This is when Constantine moved the capital from Rome to Constantinople. Eventually, Rome would be sacked by Alaric in AD 410, while Constantinople would not be sacked until the late Middle Ages.

Here are what some scholars have said about the weakness of the Western Empire compared to the Eastern.

> The East, always wealthier, was not so destitute, especially as Emperors like Constantine the Great and Constantius II had invested heavily in the eastern economy. As a result, the Eastern Empire could afford large numbers of professional soldiers and augment them with mercenaries, while the Western Roman Empire could not afford this to the same extent. Even in major defeats, the East could, certainly not without difficulties, buy off its enemies with a ransom.

> The political, economic and military control of the Eastern Empire's resources remained safe in Constantinople.... In contrast, the Western Empire was more fragmented. Its capital was transferred to Ravenna in 402 largely for defensive reasons.
>
> The Western Empire's resources were much limited, and the lack of available manpower forced the government to rely ever more on confederate barbarian troops operating under their own commanders, where the Western Empire would often have difficulties paying. In certain cases deals were struck with the leaders of barbaric mercenaries rewarding them with land, which led to the Empire's decline as less land meant there would be even less taxes to support the military.... As the central power weakened, the State gradually lost control of its borders and provinces, as well as control over the Mediterranean Sea.

The divided parts of this kingdom were noticeably different in strength. As mentioned, the Eastern Empire would survive in some capacity for hundreds of years after the West had long disappeared.

> **As you saw iron mixed with ceramic clay, they will mingle with the seed of men; but they will not adhere to one another, just as iron does not mix with clay. (Daniel 2:43)**

There is a lot of confusion about this verse, which I think is due to the English translation of the Aramaic. This section of Daniel is written in Aramaic, not Hebrew. Other translations, such as the ESV, render the underlying Aramaic phrase this way:

> As you saw the iron mixed with soft clay, so they will **mix with one another in marriage**, but they will not hold together, just as iron does not mix with clay. (emphasis added)

Instead of "mingle with the seed of men," the phrase reads, "mix with one another in marriage." So, the question is: Is the ESV capturing the intent of the Aramaic here? Let's first look at the word translated as "mingle."

The word translated as "mingle" is the Aramaic word "Arab" (ar-av), which corresponds to the Hebrew "Arab." In other words, this word, if you look it up, will be in Aramaic, and its only use is right here in Daniel, because Aramaic is very rare. However, most Aramaic words correspond directly to Ancient Hebrew words, and that is the case here. In fact, the Aramaic and Hebrew for "mingle" are even pronounced the same. The Hebrew "Arab" means: "to pledge, exchange, mortgage, engage, occupy, undertake for, give pledges, be or become surety, take on pledge, give in pledge."[71] For example, in Genesis 43:9, when Judah was begging his father to let him take Benjamin to Egypt as per Joseph's request, Judah says that he will become "surety" for Benjamin. The word "surety" is where we get the word "mingle." "I myself will be **surety** for him; from my hand you shall require him. If I do not bring him back to you and set him before you, then let me bear the blame forever" (Genesis 43:9, emphasis added).

Another example of the use of this word is in 2 Kings 18:23, where the word "pledge" is the word translated "mingle" in our passage: "Now therefore, I urge you, give a **pledge** to my master

[71] The *KJV Old Testament Hebrew Lexicon.*

the king of Assyria, and I will give you two thousand horses—if you are able on your part to put riders on them!" (2 Kings 18:23)

But the same word for "mingle" also can mean "to mix together." And in fact, of the two times it's used that way in the Bible, it is speaking of the intermarriage of Jewish and pagan tribes:

> For they have taken of their daughters for themselves, and for their sons: so that the holy **seed** have **mingled** themselves with the people of those lands: yea, the hand of the princes and rulers hath been chief in this trespass. (Ezra 9:2, emphasis added).

Here we have a very similar phrase to the one in our verse. I think this shows some precedent that the translators of the KJV believed that mingling seed was referring to intermarriage with two groups: "But they **mingled** with the Gentiles and learned their works" (Psalm 106:35).

So I think you can see that the ESV has a pretty decent rendering of this phrase when it says "mix with one another in marriage." Even if that is true, we still have to determine who "they" are, and whom "they" are trying to intermarry with.

I suggest the simple method of sentence structure and basic grammar to find out who "they" are. If we look in verse 41, we see that Daniel says the feet and toes of clay and iron represent a divided kingdom. The next three verses repeatedly refer to these two divisions of the kingdom as iron and clay. Grammatically, there is no other possible plural subject other than the separate, divided parts of the kingdom represented by the iron and clay. This is confirmed in verse 44, which says "in the days of *these kings*," making it clear that the plural subject that was in view in verse 43 must be referring to the kings of the divided kingdom in verse 41.

So, this verse is saying that the divided parts of the empire (the iron and the clay) will pledge their offspring to one another in an attempt to become strong again, but it will not work.

It would be one thing if we had to look for some obscure fulfillment of this in Roman history, but the strength of this interpretation is the unambiguous fulfillment of it in the history of Rome, which gives the interpretations a great deal more credibility. In order for this to be true, we can't just go picking any arranged marriages of emperors in Ancient Rome. Almost every senator, general, prefect, or any other person with imperial ambitions had arranged marriages to secure their legitimacy to the throne. I'm only slightly exaggerating when I say that we can't look at a single page in the entire history of Rome without reading about an arranged political marriage to solidify alliances. But we are looking for a very specific type of political marriage here. It has to be toward the very end of Rome's existence; because it is regarding the feet and toes, it has to be between the Eastern and Western Empires. In addition, the two kings of the divided kingdom need to pledge their offspring to one another for the specific purpose of trying to unify Rome and keep it from demise. That should narrow the search quite a bit.

There are two instances of this exact thing happening at the end of the Roman Empire. The first is in AD 467, only about nine years before the last Roman emperor. This is when the Vandals were posing a major threat to Rome and Leo was reigning strongly in the East. There had not been an emperor in the West for a few years because a man named Ricimer, who had been ruling behind the scenes by manipulating puppet emperors for many years, had not appointed another puppet emperor and was hoping no one would care or that people would just accept him as the default emperor. This became a problem in the Eastern Empire because of the threat of the Vandals and the imminent war with them. Leo needed to find a way to unite the divided empire to defend itself from destruction. He decided to choose an emperor of the West for the West. He chose a guy named Anthemius and sent him to the West with a big army so that Ricimer would have no choice but to agree.

Here is the marriage connection: The emperor of the east, Leo, gave his daughter, Leontia, to Anthemius's son, Marcian, to legitimize the reign of his new appointee to the West, essentially saying, "OK, East and West, we are all one big happy family now. So let's go fight the Vandals or we are all in big trouble." In addition, Anthemius also gave his only daughter, Alypia, to Ricimer, which also made Anthemius, who was a Greek-speaking foreigner to the west, acceptable to the Latin-speaking Romans, of which Ricimer had become kind of a ringleader. This plan actually might have worked, too, but the battle with the Vandals went very badly, and Anthemius would soon be killed; they would all be right back where they started.

This brings us to the second attempt to cleave together the East and the West through marriages. This time it occurred in AD 474, just two years before the last Roman Emperor, with Julius Nepos. Many people argue that Nepos was the last Roman Emperor, choosing not to count the child Romulus Augustulus, who "ruled" for about a year after Nepos was exiled. This time, Leo married off his niece to Nepos. The surname "Nepos" actually means "nephew." He took the surname "nephew" as his title, referring to his newly acquired nephew status to Leo in the East. This alone should show the importance of that marriage in the attempt to unify the East and the West. This effort to save the Roman Empire failed as well. It was just too late for Rome; too many problems were converging to cause its destruction. Just like this verse in Daniel says, these two divisions of the final kingdom did not adhere to one another, and the fall of the Western Roman Empire is placed somewhere around this time, between AD 476–480.

> **Daniel 2:44** And in the days of these kings the God of heaven will set up a kingdom which shall never be destroyed; and the kingdom shall not be left to other people; it shall break in pieces and consume all these kingdoms, and it shall stand forever.

> **Daniel 2:45** Inasmuch as you saw that the stone was cut out of the mountain without hands, and that it broke in pieces the iron, the bronze, the clay, the silver, and the gold—the great God has made known to the king what will come to pass after this. The dream is certain, and its interpretation is sure.

Here we come to the most crucial part of our study of this vision: the identification of this stone. Let's briefly recall what happened with this stone in Nebuchadnezzar's dream in verses 34–35:

> You watched while a stone was cut out without hands, which struck the image on its feet of iron and clay, and broke them in pieces. Then the iron, the clay, the bronze, the silver, and the gold were crushed together, and became like chaff from the summer threshing floors; the wind carried them away so that no trace of them was found. And the stone that struck the image became a great mountain and filled the whole earth. (Daniel 2:34–35)

So this stone strikes the statue on the feet, and it eventually grows to fill the whole earth.

A Kingdom

This stone is a kingdom (Daniel 2:44), a kingdom God will institute during the Roman Empire that will eventually grow to encompass the entire world. Some would say this has to be speaking of Jesus, not of a kingdom, because of Ephesians 2:20, which says He is a “cornerstone,” but that would offend the explicit teaching in this verse that this rock is a “kingdom” in the same way that the parts of the statue were kingdoms.

This rock is representative of what is known all throughout the Bible as the “kingdom of God.” Let’s look at a few verses to demonstrate two points:

1. Jesus Christ begins the kingdom of God in his day (during the Roman Empire).

2. The kingdom of God is supposed to start small and then grow large (typified by starting with the apostles and spreading to all those who will ever be saved).

Jesus Christ begins the kingdom of God in His day:

> But if I cast out demons by the Spirit of God, surely **the kingdom of God has come upon you. (**Matthew 12:28, emphasis added)
>
> Now at one point the Pharisees asked Jesus when the kingdom of God was coming, so he answered, “The kingdom of God is not coming with signs to be observed, nor will they say, ‘Look, here it is!’ or ‘There!**’ For indeed, the kingdom of God is in your midst**.” (Luke 17:20–21, emphasis added)
>
> And saying, “The time is fulfilled, and **the kingdom of God is at hand**. Repent, and believe in the gospel.” (Mark 1:15, emphasis added)

It should be noted here that there seems to be a present and future sense of the kingdom of God, in the sense that the ultimate fulfillment of the kingdom of God is not here or in this world, but rather in the future. But I believe it can also be shown with certainty that Jesus considered the kingdom of God to have been established with Him on earth during His teaching ministry.

The kingdom of God is supposed to start small and then grow large.

> Another parable He put forth to them, saying: "The kingdom of heaven is like a mustard seed, which a man took and sowed in his field, which indeed is the least of all the seeds; but when it is grown it is greater than the herbs and becomes a tree, so that the birds of the air come and nest in its branches." Another parable He spoke to them: "The kingdom of heaven is like leaven, which a woman took and hid in three measures of meal till it was all leavened." (Matthew 13:31–33)

These two parables describe the small and then growing large aspect of the kingdom of God. So this is, in a sense, a prophecy for all ancient peoples pointing toward a general time the Messiah will come; that is, the kingdom of God would be established sometime during the Roman Empire. This may be one reason messianic expectations were so high in Jesus' day.

At this point, we've only looked at one aspect of the argument that the revived Roman Empire idea is a modern, unbiblical tradition. We have seen that there is no reason to believe that last empire in Nebuchadnezzar's dream of the statue is speaking of an end-times kingdom. But to complete this argument, we need to study Daniel's vision of the four beasts in Daniel 7 to see for certain that these two chapters are unrelated. This will help us more clearly understand what the world will look like when the Antichrist rises to power.

Daniel's Vision of the Four Beasts—Daniel 7

In Daniel 7, Daniel has a vision of four beasts: a lion, a bear, a leopard and a "diverse beast." These beasts are identified as kings and/or kingdoms by the angel who interprets Daniel's dream starting in verse 17.

The question is which kingdoms are being referred to with these beasts.

As I said in an earlier chapter, most conservatives believe that Daniel 7 is simply a retelling of Daniel 2. In other words, the dream Nebuchadnezzar had in Daniel 2 of a multi-metal statue that represented the four kingdoms of Babylon, Medo-Persia, Greece, and Rome are again described here in Daniel 7. I don't agree with that view, but I do agree that the fourth beast in Daniel 7 is the kingdom of Antichrist.

In the traditional view, the beasts of chapter 7 are succeeded in time by the next beast. For example, the lion, the first beast (who they say represents Babylon) would be followed after much time by the bear (who they say represents Medo-Persia), since Babylon was conquered by Medo-Persia, and then the leopard (Greece) would conquer the bear after that, and so on. I believe there are significant reasons to challenge this view of the kingdoms being in temporal succession of one another.

I propose that this vision of the four beasts in Daniel 7 is not simply a picture of four kingdoms that have come and gone in the past, but rather of the four kingdoms that will be on the earth *at the same time* when the Antichrist begins his reign in the end times, which means that the fourth beast in Daniel 7 is not necessarily Rome.

Daniel 7:11–12 describes the Antichrist, who is thrown into the lake of fire after his reign is completed. Few conservatives would debate this point. However, after he is thrown into the lake of fire, the mentioning of the previous three beasts shows that they are *still around* at that time. In fact, Daniel says specifically that they are allowed to live on after that.

> I watched then because of the sound of the pompous words which the horn was speaking; I watched till the beast was slain, and its body destroyed and given to the burning flame. As for the rest of the beasts, they had their dominion taken away, yet their lives were prolonged for a season and a time. (Daniel 7:11–12)

In what sense can Neo-Babylonia or Medo-Persia be spoken of as living on after the Antichrist is destroyed? Most scholars give no compelling explanations for their presence and prolonging of their lives at this point. I will show why the contemporaneous view explains this verse, with many confirmations from the text. Additionally, several grammatical and contextual indications make it plain that these kingdoms exist at the same time in history. The following is an overview of the key points we will find in this vision as understood by what I will call the "contemporaneous beast view."

There is a dividing of the world into four parts in the time just before the Antichrist begins his rule (figure 1). The Antichrist eventually takes control of one of those four kingdoms, which has ten rulers (figure 2). He eventually conquers all four kingdoms through war and effectively rules the entire world in a new, amalgamated beast, as seen in Revelation 13:1–2 (figure 3).

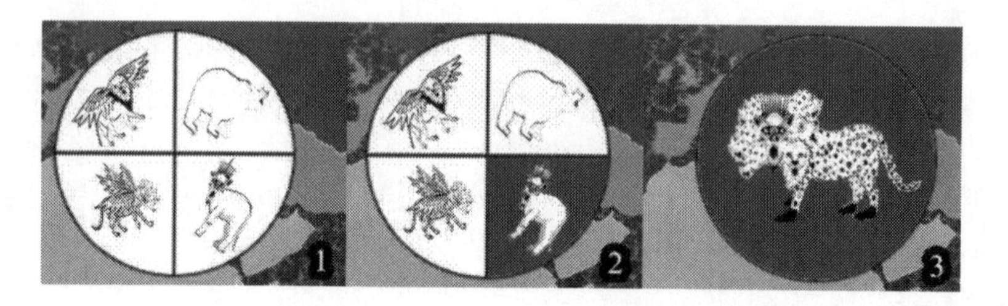

This view suggests that Daniel 11:36 and following essentially links Daniel 7 with Revelation 13. Let me explain what I mean by all that, and it may take me a minute to do so, so bear with me.

Daniel 11:36–45 describes how the Antichrist will be conquering all kinds of lands and kingdoms, then at some point, he will declare himself to be higher than God Himself in the "Holy Place" in Jerusalem. At that point, the last three and a half years of his reign will begin. But before this, he is busy making war, conquering other kingdoms and establishing his domain. This is perhaps why the book of Revelation says that one of the reasons the world marvels at the Antichrist is because of his war-making capability: "So they worshiped the dragon who gave authority to the beast; and they worshiped the beast, saying, "Who *is* like the beast? Who is able to make war with him?" (Revelation 13:4).

Arguably, the chapter that gives the most detail of the Antichrist is Revelation 13. The first two verses of that chapter say:

> Then I stood on the sand of the sea. And I saw a beast rising up out of the sea, having seven heads and ten horns, and on his horns ten crowns, and on his heads a blasphemous name. Now the beast which I saw was like a leopard, his feet were like *the feet of* a bear, and his mouth like the mouth of a lion. The dragon gave him his power, his throne, and great authority. (Revelation 13:1–2)

This is an unambiguous reference to our chapter, Daniel 7. The fact that we have a lion, a bear, and a leopard in the same place—all in the context of the Antichrist—is enough to make us pay attention, but when we see that this beast has seven heads and ten horns, a direct correlation to Daniel 7, the possibility of this being coincidental is not reasonable.

Why is this significant? If we take the beasts in Daniel 7—a lion with wings, a bear, a four-headed leopard, and a ten-horned beast—and combine them into one, we would have a seven-headed, ten-horned beast with the characteristics of a bear, a leopard, and a lion—exactly what we see in Revelation 13.

In other words, I am proposing that what we are looking at in the first few verses of Revelation 13, when a seven-headed, ten-horned lion/leopard/bear beast comes out of the sea, is the Antichrist, who is now finished with his conquest of the other three world powers and is the uncontested ruler of the world.

So, turning back to what I said earlier: The view that I promote, the contemporaneous-beast view, suggests that Daniel 11:36–45 (which describes the wars of Antichrist) essentially links Daniel 7 (the Antichrist pre-wars, in which he is only one of four powers) with Revelation 13, in which he is the uncontested ruler of all world powers. These three chapters, spread out all over the Bible, more or less provide a before, during, and after-conquests snapshot of the Antichrist.

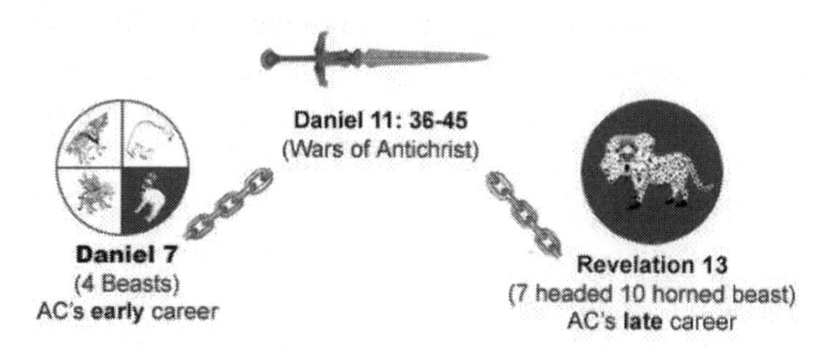

And here in Daniel 7, it gives us details on what to look for in the world just prior to and during the beginning of Antichrist's ascent to power. Daniel 11:36–45 gives what his conquests of the other powers will look like. And Revelation 13 tells what it will look like once he has gained complete control.

Let's study Daniel 7 to see if there are significant reasons to challenge the idea that this vision of Daniel is simply a mirror image of Nebuchadnezzar's vision of the statue.

> **The first was like a lion, and had eagle's wings. I watched till its wings were plucked off; and it was lifted up from the earth and made to stand on two feet like a man, and a man's heart was given to it. (Daniel 7:4)**

The traditional view has this beast being Babylon, and specifically, Nebuchadnezzar. For example, traditionalists say that wings being plucked off and its being made to stand on two feet and given a heart of a man refers to the humbling experience God gave Nebuchadnezzar in chapter 4, where the king was forced to act like an ox for several years until he recognized the sovereignty of God and then was restored to his right mind.

The picture the traditional view paints is that the lion represents Nebuchadnezzar when he was forced to act like a beast, and then the plucking of the lion's wings, making it stand on two feet, and giving it a man's heart is symbolic of God restoring Nebuchadnezzar to his right mind at the end of Daniel 4. This suggests that the reason for these four beings being described as "beasts" is because of similar situations like that of Nebuchadnezzar's. Are we to understand, then, that the kings of Medo-Persia, Greece, or Rome are also described as beasts, because they, too, were forced by God to act like beasts? If so, they were apparently not restored to sanity as Nebuchadnezzar was, since no man's heart was given to them.

The description of the first beast in Daniel 7 doesn't even fit what happened to Nebuchadnezzar in chapter 4. The clear intent in Daniel 7 is that the lion was always a lion, but was given a "man's heart" and thus changed. The lion was not restored to its natural state by the plucking of its wings and making it stand on two feet. It was permanently transformed, and the intent of the text, as we will see, is that it was a downgrade for the lion, not an upgrade. Nebuchadnezzar's situation was exactly reversed if we analyze this closely.

The traditional view also asserts things like "the winged lion is the traditional symbol for Babylon; evidence of this can be seen on the Ishtar Gate from Babylon." To start with, there is no evidence to suggest that winged lions were considered a symbol of Babylon. Lions in general, regardless of wings, were associated not with Babylon, but with the goddess Ishtar. This is partly because of the reference to her loving lions in the *Epic of Gilgamesh*, which states of Ishtar: "Thou has loved the lion, mighty in strength."

For this reason, Ishtar was often depicted with lions in sculptures and reliefs; only occasionally are the lions winged, for reasons we will get to later. This is why lions appear on the famous Ishtar gate of Babylon, because of their association with Ishtar, but Ishtar was not even the main goddess of Babylon. She, however, was, in some traditions, considered to be married to Marduk, the primary god of Babylon, thereby making Ishtar the queen of Babylon by marriage, according to those traditions.

There are other winged animals on the gate, like the bull, though most of the bulls do not have wings. In fact, the other two animals depicted on the gate (bulls and dragons) vastly outnumber the lions. There were 120 lions compared to 575 dragons and bulls. Incidentally, Nebuchadnezzar was really proud of the bulls and dragons on the front of the gate (where we won't find any lions). He even mentions them specifically in his inscription about why he built the gate, but he doesn't mention the lions at all.

All that to say that many commentators who try to make the point that winged lions are symbols of Babylon do so despite the historical evidence that winged lions are quite simply not symbols of Babylon at all, and when they do show up in Babylon, they are exceedingly rare.

People trying to make this winged lion in verse 4 be Babylon are often thinking of the so-called Lamassu. A Lamassu is a representation of a protective deity, not from Babylon but rather thousands of years before this in the Akkadian and then Assyrian kingdoms, who were enemies of Babylon. Although there are occasions when Lamassu have been depicted with lions' bodies, the vast majority are with bulls' bodies. There is some evidence that the Assyrian tradition of putting Lamassu, their protective deities, on city gates was why certain animals on other gates in later periods were given wings, as a tip of the hat to the older, Akkadian traditions regarding these protective deities.

This interpretation causes a hermeneutical problem as well. If we are going to say that we should look for a culture's symbol for itself to decipher the following beast kingdoms, then how are we to deal with the rest of the beasts? There is not a shred of evidence that, for example, the Medo-Persians symbolized themselves with a bear. I don't even think any traditional commentators try to suggest this. Nor did Greece make statues or reliefs symbolizing itself as a leopard, let alone Rome depicting itself with the odd beast that Daniel describes. If we're going to say that we can decipher the beasts/kingdoms in Daniel 7 by looking at the artwork and symbols of the kingdom in question, then it needs to be consistent.

There is a similar problem with the next point, brought up by proponents of the traditional view, which is that Nebuchadnezzar is called both a lion and an eagle in Scripture. This is the best of the point that the traditionalists have to offer in favor of their view that the four beasts of Daniel 7 are the same as the nations in Daniel 2. Even so, it should be considered that Scripture also calls Shalmaneser, the king of Assyria, a lion and an eagle in Hosea 8:1 and Jeremiah 50:17. A simple study of the usage of lions, eagles, or any other beast in Scripture reveals that they are used to designate characteristics, and are often widely interchangeable among individuals or nations—as long as the individuals or nations display the characteristics of the animal described in Scripture. For example, when used in a negative sense, lions are, among other things, strong (Proverbs 30:30), fearless (Proverbs 28:1, 30:30), stealthy (Psalm 17:12), frightening (Ezra 19:7; Hosea 11:10; Amos 3:8), destructive (1 Samuel 17:34; Micah 5:8) and territorially protective (Isaiah 31:4).

Similarly, eagles are used to depict specific characteristics of individuals or nations throughout Scripture. According to one Bible encyclopedia, it is "referred to for its swiftness of flight (Deut. 28:49; 2 Sam. 1:23), its mounting high in the air (Job 39:27), its strength (Ps. 103:5), its setting its nest in high places (Jer. 49:16), and its power of vision (Job 39:27-30)." Referred to in the article cited as a "ravenous bird," it "is a symbol of those nations whom God employs and sends forth to do a work of destruction, sweeping away whatever is decaying and putrescent (Matt. 24:28; Isa. 46:11; Ezek. 39:4; Deut. 28:49; Jer. 4:13; 48:40).[72]

So consider that when lions or eagles are used to describe kings, the imagery is used of different kings and often different kingdoms, but the unifying factor is that they are instruments of God in the judgment of Israel and display the characteristics of the animals laid out in Scripture.

Again, the traditional view would fail at applying this hermeneutic to the other three beasts. For example, there is no reference in Scripture to Alexander the Great or Greece as a leopard, or to Cyrus or Medo-Persia as a bear.

I suggest that we should attempt to interpret the first beast the same as we would the others. The most scriptural way to do that is by understanding the symbolism of the beasts by the different characteristics of that particular animal provided in Scripture.

The first was like a lion, and had eagle's wings.

A kingdom that is like a lion and has wings like an eagle suggests a strong and swift nation. Second Samuel 1:23 says:

> Saul and Jonathan were beloved and pleasant in their lives,
> And in their death they were not divided;
> They were swifter than eagles,
> They were stronger than lions. (2 Samuel 1:23)

---

[72] http://christiananswers.net/dictionary/eagle.html.

We could apply the other characteristics of these two animals to these beasts for more clarity, but the important part in terms of interpretation comes with the following lines:

I watched till its wings were plucked off; and it was lifted up from the earth and made to stand on two feet like a man, and a man's heart was given to it.

Both the wings being plucked off and the lion being forced to act like a man are to be understood as a bad thing, not a good thing, for this kingdom. The wings being plucked is pretty obvious: If the kingdom was swift like an eagle, but its wings were plucked, it would not be to the nation's advantage.

The act of giving the creature a man's heart should be understood as having its lion's heart changed into a weaker heart. Scripture is clear that a lion's heart is better than a man's with regard to boldness or fearlessness.

- And even he who is valiant, whose heart is like the heart of a lion, will melt completely. For all Israel knows that your father is a mighty man, and those who are with him are valiant men. (2 Samuel 17:10)

- The wicked flee when no one pursues, But the righteous are bold as a lion. (Proverbs 28:1)

If I was looking for this kingdom, I would be looking for one that was strong and fast, but that had its swiftness removed and that demonstrated less boldness than it once had.

And suddenly another beast, a second, like a bear. It was raised up on one side, and had three ribs in its mouth between its teeth. And they said thus to it: "Arise, devour much flesh!" (Daniel 7:5).

The next beast Daniel describes is "like a bear." In the traditional view, this is Medo-Persia, because, again those who hold the traditional view believe that this is a retelling of Daniel 2 in which the second part of the statue is indeed Medo-Persia.

As we have already noted, none of the ideas traditional-view proponents apply to the lion work for the bear. There is nothing to indicate any Medo-Persian king had a humbling experience that made him think like a beast, nor is there any indication whatsoever that the Medo-Persian empire identified itself symbolically or any other way with a bear—and there is never a reference to a Medo-Persian king as a bear in Scripture.

It was raised up on one side.

Proponents of the traditional view say that the bear being raised up on one side is symbolic of the uneven relationship between the Medes and Persians in their coalition. The Medes were initially the dominant party, but later, the Persians were the more dominant of the two parts of this empire.

Note that the phrase "raised up" here is passive; that is, the bear was raised up on one side by an outside force—not of its own doing. Much like the lion having its wings plucked and being stood up, etc., this bear is being raised up on one side by another party, probably by the group that is also ordering it to "devour much flesh." The verse says: "And they said thus to it: 'Arise, devour much flesh!'" The "they" could be a reference to the winds of the earth that stir up the sea in verse 1.

***And had three ribs in its mouth between its teeth*.**

The three ribs in the bear's mouth, according to the traditional view, represent three notable conquests of the Medo-Persian empire. But because there are more than three notable conquests of the Medo-Persian empire, there is much argument among those holding this view as to which three should be considered the most important. I, of course, don't think this has anything to do with the Medo-Persian empire, and so believe we should not concern ourselves with why this is not a perfect description of its military conquests—because it isn't.

One interesting verse is found in Hosea 13:7–8, in which God describes Himself as all of the beasts in this chapter. This is the only time these beasts are found together other than in Revelation 13, and that passage gives us an idea of what these ribs are:

> So I will be to them like a lion;
> Like a leopard by the road I will lurk;
> I will meet them like a bear deprived *of her cubs;*
> I will tear open their rib cage,
> And there I will devour them like a lion.
> The wild beast shall tear them. (Hosea 13:7–8)

The bear is described here as tearing open a rib cage, so I think the basic hermeneutic applied to the bear by the traditional view is correct: the ribs represent initial conquests by this kingdom that are three in number.

Also note that almost every time a bear is figured in Scripture, the idea of it being, as it says here, "deprived of her cubs," is mentioned. That is, the biblical bear is the most ferocious when its offspring is threatened. This is such a consistent theme that I would be surprised if the nations the bear represents are not acting out of a real or perceived sense of defense.

And they said thus to it: "Arise, devour much flesh!"

This phrase is very important, as it weakens the case that this beast represents Medo-Persia. After the conquests of Cyrus the Great and his son Cambyses II, which occurred relatively quickly and very early in the Medo-Persian history, there were two hundred years of no conquering at all, until the empire was defeated by Alexander the Great. The empire spent most of its existence simply struggling to maintain the lands that were initially conquered for it by Cyrus and his son. So, if this bear already with the main conquests in its mouth is supposed to be Medo-Persia, then it either chose not to devour any more flesh, as it was ordered to, or the image simply is not referring to the Medo-Persian Empire.

> **"After this I looked, and there was another, like a leopard, which had on its back four wings of a bird. The beast also had four heads, and dominion was given to it. (Daniel 7:6).**

The leopard with four bird wings and four heads is the Greek Empire in the traditional view. Again, this theory has the same problems as the bear, since Alexander the Great was not humbled by having his mind turned into a beast's mind. Nor is the symbol of the leopard associated with the Greek Empire; nor is Alexander the Great or Greece referred to as a leopard in the Bible. I would agree them, however, that the four wings on the leopard probably represent a very fast-moving empire.

One of the biggest problems with this view is the four heads of this beast. The traditional proponents say that these heads represent the four generals whom Alexander the Great gave his empire to after he died. The traditional view, then, has Scripture attributing the fast and ferocious conquests of the Grecian Empire to the four generals; no mention of Alexander is present. This is problematic to say the least. Even if we were to assume that Alexander was somehow involved—perhaps he was the torso—to give such prominence to the generals is inconsistent with history and with the way Scripture uses the head/kingdoms motif.

How does Scripture speak of leopards? They tear into pieces (Jeremiah 5:6), they are swift (Habakkuk 1:8), and they lie in wait for their prey (Jeremiah 5:6, Hosea 13:7).

We are looking for an exceedingly fast coalition of four end-times kings or kingdoms or even four leaders of the same kingdom. And, because of the consistent use in Scripture, this kingdom will have some quality that can be described as "lying in wait" or "being patient before striking."

Mention of the leopard is found only about six times in Scripture, and the only time the term seems to apply to any nation or king is in Revelation 13, where we see that all four of the beasts have been combined as they rise out of the sea for the final three and a half years of Antichrist's rule, suggesting again that we are to understand these kingdoms in Daniel 7 as somehow being represented again all the way in Revelation 13.

> **Daniel 7:7** "After this I saw in the night visions, and behold, a fourth beast, dreadful and terrible, exceedingly strong. It had huge iron teeth; it was devouring, breaking in pieces, and trampling the residue with its feet. It *was* different from all the beasts that *were* before it, and it had ten horns.
>
> **Daniel 7:8** I was considering the horns, and there was another horn, a little one, coming up among them, before whom three of the first horns were plucked out by the

> roots. And there, in this horn, *were* eyes like the eyes of a man, and a mouth speaking pompous words.

Here the traditional view has Rome in sight. The reasons for this—strength and fearfulness because of its might—are very general and can apply to any of the previous kingdoms. Any world empire would be able to claim these characteristics. The idea that Rome was "different" from the previous kingdoms can also apply to any kingdom on the list, depending we how you define "different."

There are major differences in the fourth empire described here and the last empire described in the statue vision back in Daniel 2. For instance, in this verse, the strength of the empire is clearly the main focus; not a hint of weakness is detected. Contrast that with the last part of the last empire of Daniel 2, in which the Bible spends verse after verse describing the divided nature and inherent weakness of that kingdom. I would call that a very big difference! The kingdom in Daniel 2 is divided and weak, and the kingdom in Daniel 7 is described as invincible.

The main point seen as the clincher for the traditional view is the reference to the ten horns, which is said to correspond to the ten toes in Daniel 2. But I beg the reader to realize that there is no mention of ten toes in Daniel 2. That idea has been read back into the text by people who assume these two chapters are the same.

In chapter 2, the feet and toes are one unit, a fact easily demonstrated not just by the descriptions of them being one unit in the text, but also by the rock striking the feet, not the toes, in order to destroy the statue. If the biblical writer wanted to make a big deal out of the ten toes, he would have said, "By the way, there are ten toes," but he does not. There is no mention of the number of toes in the text. For example, I believe we are supposed to pay attention to the number of ribs in the bear's mouth (three), and, in the next chapter, the number of horns on the ram's head, or even the number of horns on this beast's head (ten). But when a number is not mentioned, we shouldn't read one into the text. No one tries to draw attention to the ten fingers on the hands of the statue that represents Medo-Persia, because there is no correlation there; it takes the analogy too far. We wouldn't note that there are two eyes and ears on the head, either. When the Bible is silent, we should be too.

That being said, I do have some agreement with the traditional view at this point, in that I think the kingdom the Antichrist comes from will have ten kings because of this passage in Daniel 7 and because of its interpretation by the angel, which we will get to later. The Antichrist indeed seems to arise from some kind of ten-nation/king confederacy, and he will subdue three of them before ultimately talking over the whole organization.

Two grammatical clues in this verse support the overall premise that the four beasts are contemporaneous and not successive. The first is the use of the word "before" in verse 7: "It *was* different from all the beasts that *were* before it."

The word "before" here is the Aramaic word *qodam,* which is only used in a spatial sense and never in a temporal sense. It is never used in the time sense, like "he tied his shoes before he ran." It is only used in the sense of being in front of something, like "I put some food before the king."

One example of how this word is used is in Daniel 2:25:

> Then Arioch quickly brought Daniel before the king, and said thus to him, "I have found a man of the captives of Judah, who will make known to the king the interpretation." (Daniel 2:25)

A different word would be used to speak of something happening before something else in time. So when the verse says, "It *was* different from all the beasts that were **before** it," it must mean that the other beasts are spatially in front of it, indicating that these beasts must be on the earth at the same time.

This brings us to the second grammatical clue in this verse. The phrase, "trampling the residue with its feet," also supports the idea that these beasts are contemporaneous.

Biblical scholar Charles Cooper says the following on this point:

> The importance of the translation of this verse is evident by examining several Bible translations:
>
> A fourth beast, dreadful and terrifying and extremely strong; and it had large iron teeth. It devoured and crushed and trampled down the remainder with its feet. (NASB)
>
> A fourth beast, terrifying and dreadful and exceedingly strong. It had great iron teeth; it devoured and broke in pieces and stamped what was left with its feet. (ESV)
>
> a fourth beast, dreadful and terrible, and strong exceedingly; and it had great iron teeth: it devoured and broke in pieces, and stamped the residue with the feet of it. (1895-KJV)
>
> a fourth beast—terrifying and frightening and very powerful. It had large iron teeth; it crushed and devoured its victims and trampled underfoot whatever was left. (NIV)
>
> The reader should discern that the translations, with the exception of the NIV, place the final clause as the object of

all three verbs. Does "what was left" go with the final verb to stamp or with all three verbs: to devour, to break in pieces, and to stamp? The answer to this question along with the question regarding the meaning of the clause "what was left" support our contention that the four kings/kingdoms of Daniel 7 reign upon the earth at the same time. If the clause "what was left" applies only to the verb to stamp, we would have to conclude that the clause refers to the things the beast did not devour or break in pieces. In other words, "what was left" is everything else the beast is not able to devour or break in pieces. If the beast could not "eat" it or "break" it, he stamped on it.

The other option is to take "what was left" as the object of all three verbs: to devour, to break in pieces, and to stamp, which is reflected in most translations. Taken in this sense, "what was left" represents everything the first three beasts do not control. In other words, the four kings/kingdoms divided the world up between them. The lion-king, the bear-king, the leopard king, and the diverse-king each get a fourth. In context, "what was left" is best taken to refer to that part of the earth that did not fall under the control of the first three beasts/kings/kingdoms.[73]

Daniel 7: 9–11

Daniel 7:9 I watched till thrones were put in place, And the Ancient of Days was seated; His garment *was* white as

[73] Charles Cooper. "Daniel 2 and 7: Equal or Not Equal Part 4", n.d. http://www.prewrathrapture.com/Daniel%202%20and%207%20-%20Equal%20or%20Not%20Equal%20-%20Part%204.pdf.

snow, And the hair of His head *was* like pure wool. His throne *was* a fiery flame, its wheels a burning fire;

Daniel 7:10 A fiery stream issued And came forth from before Him. A thousand thousands ministered to Him; Ten thousand times ten thousand stood before Him. The court was seated, And the books were opened.

Daniel 7:11 I watched then because of the sound of the pompous words which the horn was speaking; I watched till the beast was slain, and its body destroyed and given to the burning flame.

Daniel now shifts his attention to a new character in the vision: the Ancient of Days. This is a reference to YHWH, though the same description is applied to Jesus in Revelation. Later we will see the Son of Man whom Jesus identified with interacting with the Ancient of Days.

Daniel is now going to watch the Ancient of Days destroy the beast with the little horn by giving it to the burning flame. These verses are very important for our discussion, because they correspond directly to events in the book of Revelation. If we compare the two books, we will see that Daniel is giving us very specific information about the timing of the events being described in this chapter.

Let's start with the first phrase: "I watched till thrones were put in place."

I will quote from the last part of Revelation 19 to the first part of Revelation 20. First you will see the Antichrist is cast into the lake of fire, just as it happens in our passage:

> Then the beast was captured, and with him the false prophet who worked signs in his presence, by which he deceived those who received the mark of the beast and those who worshiped his image. These two were cast alive into the lake of fire burning with brimstone. (Revelation 19:20)

Then we read that thrones are set up after that, which corresponds with Daniel as well:

> And I saw thrones, and they sat on them, and judgment was committed to them. (Revelation 20:4a)

This shows that there is a direct chronological match with the events of Daniel 7 and Revelation 19 and 20.

The comparisons to the time just before the millennial reign of Christ are very important, and Daniel will continue to make unambiguous references to it. One reason I want to address this is because I think it helps to explain the next verse.

> **As for the rest of the beasts, they had their dominion taken away, yet their lives were prolonged for a season and a time. (Daniel 7:12)**

"As for the rest of the beasts": There is no doubt that the other beasts of Daniel 7 are in view here—that is, the lion, the bear and the leopard. Their dominion is taken away, but their lives are prolonged for a time.

This verse is very difficult to get around for those who still hold the traditional view, because the other beasts are long gone by this point. Stephen Miller, author of the commentary on Daniel for the *New American Commentary* who holds to the traditional view, offers the following to explain this most serious problem:

> How could these beasts lose their authority and still exist? The explanation is that their dominance ceased, but they continued to live because they were absorbed into the next empire. For example, Greece was conquered by Rome; and although Greek dominance came to an end, the nation continued to live by being absorbed into another one of the earthly kingdoms, the Roman Empire.[74]

So according to Miller, when Daniel says "As for the rest of the beasts, they had their dominion taken away, yet their lives were prolonged for a season and a time," he means that there would still be Neo-Babylonian or Medo-Persian blood on the earth in the last days. This presumes that the Bible sees kingdoms in a purely ethnic sense, which is very difficult when dealing with kingdoms like the Romans, who were very ethnically diverse.

I have another explanation for this problem. After the Antichrist is destroyed at Armageddon, there will still be people and indeed nations on earth who will populate the thousand-year period after the sheep and goat judgment. This has explicit biblical support. We know there will be specifically identifiable nations in the Millennium. For example, in Zechariah 14:16–19, Egypt is mentioned. In fact, that same passage specifically states that some of the nations that were a part of the final battles would be serving the Lord during this time: "And it shall come to pass, that **every one that is left of all the nations** which came against Jerusalem shall even go up from year to year to worship the King" (emphasis added)

So the nations involved in this vision are allowed to continue into the Millennium, based on the context. This is very difficult to say

---

[74] Stephen B. Miller. "Daniel." In *New American Commentary,* 18, 206, n.d.

of Neo-Babylonia or Medo-Persia, but it makes sense if these four beasts are last-days kingdoms controlled by the Antichrist.

For a complete study on this chapter in Daniel, see my commentary on the book of Daniel entitled *Daniel—A Commentary* available on www.Amazon.com.

I hope readers will consider the possibility that Daniel 2 and Daniel 7 are not speaking of the same events. While I don't regard this as an absolutely crucial doctrine to understanding the end times as a whole, I do think that by believing them to be the same, thereby causing a revived Roman Empire view to exist, we set ourselves up to be confused when the Antichrist does appear.

Appendix B

Two Horns Like a Lamb

In this book, I have detailed many reasons why the actions of the False Prophet seem to suggest that he is attempting to make people believe he is the return of Elijah, the prophet. I have also noted that many modern prophecy students, in their attempts to force Islamic eschatology into biblical eschatology, have suggested that the False Prophet is the Islamic version of Jesus, who is called "Isa." The passage they refer to as supporting this claim is Revelation 13:11, which says: "Then I saw another beast coming up out of the earth, and he had two horns like a lamb and spoke like a dragon" (Revelation 13:11).

They argue that because the False Prophet is said to have "two horns like a lamb," he is attempting to imitate Jesus, who is often referred to as "The Lamb."

I believe the correct way to interpret this passage is in light of Jesus' warnings about false prophets in Matthew 7:15, which says "Beware of false prophets, who come to you in sheep's clothing, but, inwardly, they are ravenous wolves" (Matthew 7:15).

Jesus said that false prophets would come in sheep's clothing, but would, inwardly, be like wolves. In this passage, it seems clear that Jesus is not using the sheep imagery to refer to Himself but to suggest that false prophets would act as though they are meek and harmless like lambs. He is, essentially, using the sheep imagery the same way He does in many other places in Scripture[75]—in a generic sense, to speak of people who are meek and harmless.

This seems to be confirmed by the context of Revelation 13:11, because it goes on to contrast the False Prophet's looking like a lamb with his speech, which is like a dragon: "Then I saw another beast coming up from the earth. He had two horns like a lamb, but[76] was speaking like a dragon" (NET).

This is virtually the same illustration Jesus gave about false prophets: They dress up like sheep but are really wolves. However, in this case, a dragon is used instead of wolves, which is probably to link the speech of the False Prophet to the satanic doctrine he will be teaching.

The idea that the False Prophet has two horns like a lamb is to be understood as him trying to seem like a genuine lamb, because this is the normal number of horns for a lamb which they grow just after they are weaned. In other words, the concept of having two horns like a lamb is to be connected with the idea of having "sheep's clothing." This has been noted in many Bible commentaries, such as the theologian Johann Peter Lange's *Commentary on the Holy Scriptures: Critical, Doctrinal, and Homiletical, Volume 10*, which says:

> We do not translate, like **the** lamb.... The two horns, therefore, are not to be placed in the category of a defect, in accordance with Ebrard: the Beast (ver. 11) has but two horns, and is thus distinguished, as a natural sheep.

---

[75] John 21:15–16 is notable because it shows that lambs and sheep are interchangeable.

[76] Net Bible footnote for the word "but": "Here καί (kai) has been translated as 'but' to indicate the contrast present in this context."

In addition to this, I draw the reader's attention to how Jesus used the term "false prophets" in the Olivet Discourse, which almost certainly has the False Prophet of Revelation 13 in mind:

> Then, if anyone says to you, "Look, here is the Christ!" or "There!," do not believe it. For false christs and false prophets will rise and show great signs and wonders to deceive, if possible, even the elect. (Matthew 24:23–24)

Here, Jesus is contrasting the false prophets who show "great signs," (the same Greek phrase John uses to describe the False Prophet's signs in Revelation) with false christs. The fact that Jesus makes a clear distinction between these last-days false christs and false prophets makes it very unlikely that the False Prophet will also be a false christ, because it seems clear he is warning of two distinct types of last-days deceivers, and not one deceiver who will be both a false christ and a false prophet. In fact, this gives all the more weight to the thesis of this book, because the False Prophet of Revelation 13 is using his "great signs" to promote the worship of the Antichrist, which, if we follow the pattern in the Olivet Discourse, means that the Antichrist is a false messiah or false christ.

More From Chris White

Available at Amazon

Available at Amazon

You can subscribe to Chris White's Bible Prophecy Talk podcast at the following links:

Bible Prophecy Talk RSS:
http://feeds.feedburner.com/bibleprophecytalk/NcwG
Bible Prophecy Talk Itunes:
http://itunes.apple.com/us/podcast/bible-prophecy-talk/id482171080

Sign up for Chris' mailing list on the front page of his website: http://BibleProphecytalk.com

You can contact him directly at chris@BibleProphecytalk.com

If you enjoyed this book please consider reviewing it on Amazon. Every review helps the message of this book reach more people.

Manufactured by Amazon.ca
Bolton, ON